BRING BACK THE POLL TAX!

THE GOP WAR ON VOTING RIGHTS

BRING BACK THE POLL TAX!
THE GOP WAR ON VOTING RIGHTS

by
Earl Ofari Hutchinson

MIDDLE PASSAGE PRESS

Bring Back the Poll Tax!—The GOP War on Voting Rights

Copyright © 2021 Earl Ofari Hutchinson
All rights reserved including the right of reproduction in whole or in part in any form.

Printed in the United States

Published by
Middle Passage Press
5517 Secrest Drive
Los Angeles, California 90043

Indexed by Middle Passage Press Index Services
Designed by Alan Bell

Publisher's Cataloging-in-Publication Data
Names: Hutchinson, Earl Ofari.
Title: Bring back the poll tax! The GOP war on voting rights / Earl Ofari Hutchinson.
Description: Los Angeles, CA : Middle Passage Press, 2021. | Includes bibliographical references and index.
Identifiers: LCCN | ISBN 9781881032502 (pbk.)
Subjects: LCSH: Voting Rights Act of 1965 (United States). | Election law — United States. | Suffrage — United States — History — 20th century. | Suffrage — United States — History — 21st century. | Voting — United States. | BISAC: POLITICAL SCIENCE / American Government / National. | POLITICAL SCIENCE — Political Ideologies — Conservatism & Liberalism. | POLITICAL SCIENCE / Political Ideologies / Democracy.
Classification: LCC JK1846.H88 2021 | DDC 324.6 H—dc23
LC record available at https://lccn.loc.gov/

Library of Congress Control Number:
Middle Passage Press, Los Angeles, California

TABLE OF CONTENTS

1	Introduction
7	Dead Men Tell GOP Lies
16	The GOP Defender of the Vote Realm
23	Show Me the Money and the Constitution
32	Color Vote Suppression Green
39	Kicking Vote Suppression into High Gear
45	"Conditionally Suspect" The Never-Ending War Against the Voting Rights Act
60	Back to the Edmund Pettus Bridge
67	Plotting to take Back the White House and Much More
71	The Felon Voting Ban is a Black Ban
79	The Grave Danger to Democrats in 2022

83	Then There's the Electoral College
89	The Racial Vote Suppression Card
94	Obama Showed the Way
101	Conclusion
105	Appendix I Key Provisions of the Voting Rights Act of 1965
109	Appendix II 10 Key Provisions of HR 1 "For the People Act"
115	Notes
123	Bibliography
125	Index
128	About Earl Ofari Hutchinson

BRING BACK THE POLL TAX!
THE GOP WAR ON VOTING RIGHTS

INTRODUCTION

Former President Trump wasted no time making the claim that had practically been his mantra and that of the GOP for decades. A few days after he was ousted from the Oval Office by Democratic presidential opponent Joe Biden, Trump tweeted:

"In certain swing states, there were more votes than people who voted, and in big numbers. Does that not really matter? Stopping Poll Watchers, voting for unsuspecting people, fake ballots and so much more. Such egregious conduct. We will win!"
—Donald J. Trump (@realDonaldTrump)
November 23, 2020"

Trump managed to beat the hat trick with this tweet.

He spewed all the by now standard talking points, hit notes, and flat-out lies that he and the GOP relentlessly peddled about alleged voting fraud. There were more votes than voters. There were poll watchers who suddenly vanished and were unable to catch the alleged cheaters. There were phantom, dummy, and paid voters who stuffed the ballot boxes.

The jewel in the crown of Trump/GOP vote fraud lies was this: There were loads of fake ballots. Who did Trump think gamed the system so shamelessly and blatantly to steal the election from him? Who else, but the Democrats? Trump's phony vote fraud claim was in effect the official marching order for packs of GOP governors, GOP controlled state legislators, GOP house reps and senators, legions of GOP political action groups, conservative talking heads, and bloggers in the states and nationally to go on the attack.

The attack culminated in the January 6, 2021, Capitol Building assault that claimed lives, sent legislators scurrying in fear for their lives, and caused tens of thousands of dollars in property damage to the Capitol Building.

* * * * *

Former Senate Majority Leader Mitch McConnell made the vote fraud lie quasi-official when he like Trump wasted no time in cheerleading Trump's bogus claim that Trump was still President. In a speech on the Senate floor, November 5, 2020, McConnell egged Trump on in pushing his fraudulent claim that he was cheated out of the Oval Office.

He harped that Trump was "100 percent within his rights" to scream that there were "irregularities" in the voting.

McConnell eventually and very grudgingly conceded that Biden did indeed win the presidency. That didn't end the little GOP vote fraud charade. McConnell made clear that he would do everything he could to rein in, maybe sabotage was the more accurate term, Biden's legislative initiatives.

The Trump/GOP phony canard of vote fraud, in truth, was a rehash of the same warmed-over attacks that the GOP had ruthlessly made for two decades since the Bush-Gore presidential debacle in 2000. That was to bend, twist, manipulate, massage, and out and out scrap legal voting rights laws and standards in the states.

Within months, the GOP governors and GOP-controlled legislators outdid themselves. They proposed and tried to ram through dozens of vote restriction laws. The proposals were the by now usual assorted stuff of everything from airtight voter IDs to closing polling places in predominantly minority neighborhoods.

The GOP-dominated states weren't the only ones who got into the vote suppression act. There was much evidence that some major corporations and business interests kicked in more than a few dollars to bankroll the GOP vote suppression campaign. The Democrats at every turn, and with each new GOP ploy, screamed foul They filed, and threatened, lawsuits in several states, staged legislative walkouts in states such as Texas and Wisconsin, and proposed HR 1.

The House passed bill was fittingly named as a deliberate "take that" to the GOP, "For the People Act."

The bill would impose uniform standards on federal voting, automatic voter registration, allow two weeks of early voting, make it harder to boot voters from the voter rolls, and most telling, it would give felons the right to vote across the board. The House passed the bill in March 2021. To no surprise, not one Republican House member backed the bill. GOP senators quickly followed suit and declared war on the bill the moment it was introduced in the Senate.

The unmistakable message from the GOP vote repression shenanigans was don't even think about such a bill having a ghost of a chance to get any GOP support. McConnell frothed on Fox News that the bill was tantamount to a federal power grab of elections. He wasn't finished. In a follow-up tweet, on March 24, he was even blunter, "Democrats' H.R. 1 would leave elections more vulnerable to cheating, send taxpayer dollars to subsidize campaigns, and would turn the bipartisan Federal Election Commission into a Democrat-controlled partisan body. It's not about protecting voting. It's about rigging the system."

* * * * *

The two-decade plus GOP assault on universal, free, and open-ended voting for all in America is a deadly game of more than just one party's mean-spirited effort to squeeze maximum political gain for itself out of the voting process. It is a brutal, frontal, assault on the spirit and meaning of the democratic voting process. It is a radical realteration of the established premise of voting in a democratic society—the hallowed rule of one person, one vote. It is in every sense a war on the American voting rights system and process.

Attorney General Merrick Garland vowed to use every weapon at the Justice Department's disposal to fight back. In June 2021, he announced that the department would radically beef up its vote enforcement unit and vigorously prosecute those who threaten and intimidate election workers. He also pledged to ramp up the Civil Rights Division's enforcement staff. Said Garland, the department would "investigate and promptly prosecute" any threats that violate federal law and committed to partnering with other federal agencies to combat disinformation surrounding elections, which "intentionally tries to suppress the vote." He'll need to do all that and much more to make even the faintest dent on the wall of voter suppression laws the GOP has busily passed in state after state.

In *Bring Back the Poll Tax!—The GOP War on Voting Rights,* Political analyst Earl Ofari Hutchinson presents a grim and gloomy assessment of how, why, and by what means the GOP has waged a ruthless, no-holds-barred war to massively restrict voting in America. Hutchinson surveys the history of the ploys, laws, and barriers the GOP has thrown up. He assesses the history of voting rights suppression and disenfranchisement of Blacks and minorities from the days of the Jim Crow poll taxes and literacy tests to the non-stop GOP assault on the 1965 Voting Rights Act.

Bring Back the Poll Tax!—The GOP War on Voting Rights presents a comprehensive analysis of the fact and fiction of vote fraud in America. Hutchinson details the steps that are, have, and can be taken to combat the GOP's bogus voter suppression scare campaign.

Hutchinson sounds a clarion call that nothing less than the right of every citizen to fully enjoy the fruit of America's democratic political process is on the line in this high-stakes war. *Bring Back the Poll Tax!—The GOP War on Voting Rights* is a primer on what and how citizens can fight to preserve their most fundamental American right. That's their right to vote.

CHAPTER 1

DEAD MEN TELL GOP LIES

Michigan voter Roberto Garcia got the unpleasant shock of his life at the close of the presidential election in November 2020. He found out that he was one of 10,000 or so deceased Michigan voters who voted. That is who voted for Biden.

He was called out by name by the local Michigan GOP. The claim of Garcia's death fit in with Trump's charge that the Democrats dredged up hordes of dead people from the cemeteries and crematoriums to vote for Biden. *Fox News* shill Tucker Carlson quickly latched onto the claim and cited it as fact. The inference was that a "dead" Roberto Garcia and thousands more of the dearly departed in Michigan were dumped on the voting rolls by cheating Democrats to vote for Biden. If so, then the Democrats could empty the cemeteries in the other states that swung to Biden.

The claim, even by the GOP's abominably low standards, was so incredible that investigators easily and quickly debunked it. A beaming and very much alive Garcia fittingly had the final word. He posed in his yard holding a gigantic Biden-Harris sign. He couldn't resist adding: "I'm definitely alive and I definitely voted for Biden!"

As for Carlson, he ate crow again, and offered yet another shame-faced apology, saying that he was "duped" by the Trump camp into reporting the lie that a supposed "dead" Georgian also voted. Like Garcia, he also turned out to be very much alive. Like Garcia, he voted for Biden.

*****

The GOP's dead person vote myth though pitiable and laughable has been often trotted out as one of its vote fraud canons. Every one of them has been painstakingly investigated to determine if there is anything to the charge. NYU's Brennan Center for

Justice has taken the lead in debunking the GOP's vote fraud lies. The Center in countless reports has found that that deliberate, designed vote fraud is virtually nonexistent in state and federal elections.

It put the incident rate of actual larcenous vote fraud at between 0.0003 percent and 0.0025 percent. This is not to say that voting mistakes and errors don't occur. They do. However, they can be attributed in almost all instances to something that can never be purged. That's human error, clerical errors, and sloppy or erroneous data matching.

The Center drove the point of the absurdity of the claim home with the proverbial quip that one stands a better chance of being struck by lightning than getting away with or even attempting to impersonate another voter at the polls. One study found a total of 30 impersonation vote fraud cases in fourteen years from 2000 to 2014. This is out of more than 1 billion ballots cast. Studies found there were almost no prosecutions for impersonation vote fraud.

Even more telling is the study that noted the likelihood of where vote fraud when it occurred was likely to come from. The accuser was almost always the loser of a race. The other big, but favored GOP lie, is the Democrats' herd packs of illegal, ineligible workers in the U.S. to the polls to vote Democrat. The Government Accounting Office, Columbia University, the Washington Post, and even the Republican National Lawyers Association, found little to support this perennial GOP allegation.

GOP officials dismiss these studies as simply more partisan propaganda by Democrats, liberals, and Democratic-leaning think tank researchers and the press. The GOP insists they have an ax to grind by downplaying alleged widespread vote fraud.

Vote fraud cases as a result almost always end up in the courts. The GOP's record here in trying to make the case for vote fraud has not been much better.

Several federal district courts have ruled that the strict

photo ID laws in Texas, North Carolina, Wisconsin, and Indiana, were racially discriminatory. There have been all of two convictions under the law out of tens of millions of votes in elections in these

states. Even when vote suppressing GOP state officials claim to know of hundreds of voter fraud cases and demand the right to prosecute the offenders, the results have been embarrassing. Kansas is a typical example.

In November 2012, Kansas Secretary of State Kris Kobach got the legislature to grant him special power to prosecute voter fraud. He claimed to know a hundred cases. He brought six prosecutions and won four. Overall, prosecutors have filed 14 vote fraud cases in 22 states out of 84 million votes cast. The prosecution rate amounted to a whopping 0.00000017 percent fraud rate.

In a bitter irony, a few years later Kobach's tenure as chair of Trump's so-called Presidential Advisory Commission on Election Integrity, ended abruptly in 2018. The Commission was disbanded by, yes, Trump. Why? Because the states said no to giving any credence to the Committee's vote fraud witch hunt.

The Department of Justice fared even worse when it scoured for cases of federal election fraud presumably to prosecute during the 2002 and 2004 federal elections, it found 0.00000013 percent of ballots cast were fraudulent. The SCOTUS is packed with Trump-friendly justices. These justices would be the most likely to find something to hang a phony vote fraud hat on. Trump got nowhere with them when he demanded the high court toss the results of the 2020 election based on fraud. This was even too much for the court. In a terse ruling in December 2020, the court tossed out his lawsuit that not surprisingly was backed by 18 GOP states attorneys general.

* * * * *

Trump and the GOP were unfazed. The GOP-controlled state legislatures simply doubled down with a fresh wave of vote suppression proposals. There were two narratives running side by side with their assault. The first was the GOP's contention that the supposed widespread vote fraud was almost exclusively among African American voters in the big, urban areas such as Philadelphia, Detroit, Milwaukee, and Atlanta. The legal briefs filed in the courts by Texas and the GOP run states that backed Trump's contention of widespread vote fraud concentrated almost entirely on the same cities with heavy minority populations in the swing states of Michigan, Wisconsin, and potentially, Texas.

The GOP understood that most Blacks in these cities are rock-solid Democrats. So, it was not so much contesting their party loyalty or affiliation that was the issue. It was the numbers turn out that was the GOP worry. The GOP banked heavily on a lower turnout among African American urban voters. Any ramp-up in the Black vote for Democrats could offset the traditional GOP majority in the predominantly white suburbs and rural areas in these states.

The combination of skilled voter education, registration, and drive with the deep loathing of Trump by Blacks provided the perfect storm for a greater than usual voter turnout in urban areas in 2020. Trump got a higher percentage of the overall vote in the states he lost. But he lost because many more people went to the polls in the urban areas. He lost in these areas by 13.2 million votes, compared with 11.1 million in 2016.

The GOP's deliberate targeting of Black voters in the urban areas in the swing states wasn't lost on voting rights advocates, "They are directly attacking Black voters and voters of color that live in these cities," says U.S. Associate Attorney General Vanita Gupta, "And I think the comparison of cities versus neighboring counties demonstrates the degree to which this is in a lot of ways reminiscent of Jim Crow voting exclusions, where they are seeking after the fact to undermine or discount Black voters."

One judge on the Wisconsin Supreme Court made the same point when Trump attorneys challenged the ballots in Milwaukee and Dane (Madison) counties, the state's two largest urban centers. Judge Jill Karofsky told Trump lawyers, "In your lawsuit what you have done here is target the vote of 250,000 people—not statewide, but in two of our 72 counties that have diverse populations, because they are urban, and because they vote Democratic. This lawsuit ... smacks of racism."

* * * * *

The not so thinly disguised racist-tinged fear that Trump stoked among his base, was that they were in mortal danger of losing their long-standing political and economic power and privilege. Their fight to preserve power was far more than a fight over the usual old-time cultural war issues—abortion, gay rights, gay marriage, and school prayer. This was hard down in the trenches' political warfare over maintaining GOP political dominance.

The cruder far-rightist groups, hectored by Trump, repeatedly voiced that fear, and made clear they were determined to do something about it. They engaged in countless marches, demonstrations, harangues, harassment, and ultimately the mass assault on the Capitol Building, January 6. 2021 Trump made no pretense about his aim when he shouted to a mostly white crowd his usual bluster in the moments before the riot, "This is our country. And you know this, and you see it, but they are trying to take it from us through rigging, fraud, deception, and deceit."

Hard right long-time top mouthpiece, Rush Limbaugh, went one better. He flatly said, "I see more and more people asking what in the world do we have in common with the people who live in, say, New York." It would be a bad mistake to think that this was just the sensationalist, audience-grabbing antic of an ultra-right talk show instigator. Trump doubled down on this theme when he told a campaign crowd in Valdosta, Georgia December 5, 2020 (population 56,457), that the Democrats were trying to "steal" the election.

The Overwhelming Majority of Republicans across all income, gender, and professional groups bought into it some surveys found up to three-fourths of Republican voters agreed. This was about the same percentage of Republicans who bought into Trump's long-standing Birther claim that Obama was not an American citizen, and therefore was ineligible (and in the minds of many unfit) to be president.

There was a third reason why the voter fraud scam has played so well among Republicans. It serves a hard-edged, calculated political purpose. That is as an organizing tool to rally and motivate GOP voters to turn out in greater numbers on Election Days.

There's yet a fourth reason the GOP vote fraud ploy has had so much currency. It touches deeply the American sense of fair play. Many Americans still remember when elections were bought and paid for, yes rigged, especially in big cities and rural areas, and especially the South. A small clique of party bosses would handpick candidates and a small army on the payroll of party loyalists, hacks, and bagmen would fan out on Election Day with money, favors, and even intimidation to ensure that thousands of voters dutifully voted for the "chosen candidate."

Election corruption and manipulated elections were the rule in these places. So, by continually harping on the notion of widespread vote fraud, the GOP can pose as the American man on the white horse battling for fair and honest voting. This coats their vote fraud scam with a veneer of plausibility, credibility, and integrity. What could be racist about wanting to ensure fair elections? They simply claim to have the noblest of aims.

There was a revealing exchange on CBS between newly minted Georgia U.S. senator Raphael Warnock and Georgia state senator Butch Miller over Georgia's ultra-restrictive voting rights bill the GOP legislature passed in March 2021. The CBS moderator didn't even get the question of racism out of his mouth about whether their racist intent, To those who call it Jim Crow 2.0 or Jim Crow in a suit and tie, you say—BUTCH MILLER: That is just sad that someone would stoop to that type of name-calling. We want everybody to have a chance to vote.

In every lawsuit, challenge, and legislative initiative the GOP has initiated, one will never find any mention of race. The legislation is solely about defending and preserving voter fairness.

Trump was aware of the blitz the GOP made in the courts and through state organizations to vote suppress. He, and GOP shills, in the conservative media, have badgered many into buying the myth of massive fraud and elections stolen by the Democrats. Yet, there is not a word from the supposed protectors of voting integrity and honesty about the very real legacy and history of vote suppression, let alone the out and out near century-long racial disenfranchisement of Blacks in the South. A history that is very much still alive and well in more than a few places in America.

CHAPTER 2

THE GOP DEFENDER OF THE VOTE REALM

A week after the 2020 presidential election in mid-November 2021, USA Today took Trump and the GOP's claims of massive vote fraud so seriously that its editors worked closely with a team of vote experts and investigators to examine ten of the claims the GOP made about vote fraud in the 2020 presidential election. Here are four of the vote fraud allegations that they examined.

Claim: Ballots were found in drainage ditches in Pennsylvania and that's evidence of election fraud by Democrats.

Fact check: There were no ballots found in a ditch. There were nine military ballots incorrectly discarded in a dumpster—seven of which were cast for Trump—but the incident was found to be an error by a contractor. The Pennsylvania secretary of state stated that the situation was not intentional fraud.

Claim: Thousands of voters in Michigan cast a ballot under the names of deceased people."

Fact check: The claim that 14,000 dead people in Wayne County, Michigan, voted in the 2020 election is false. The list has been investigated and it was found that some individuals on the list were either still alive, or not living in Michigan. Other examples cited were the date of birth errors. Ballots cast by dead people in Michigan are rejected and there is no evidence of fraud.

Claim: Ballots in Phoenix marked with Sharpies were disqualified

Fact check: There is no evidence that tabulating machines in Arizona cannot read ballots filled out with a Sharpie. The Maricopa County Elections Department confirmed that Sharpies are preferred for filling out ballots. Arizona Secretary of State Katie Hobbs also confirmed that ballots marked with Sharpie pens would be counted.

Claim: Video shows ballots for Trump being burned in Virginia Beach, Virginia.

Fact check: Virginia Beach officials confirmed that the ballots are sample ballots and are not real.

USA Today's editor-in-chief explained that the debunking of the GOP vote fraud claims was by no mean a hatchet job. He made it clear that vote fraud is a serious enough issue and that it is "poison for democracy, damaging everyone and promised to "root out fraud and report the truth." Yet, the fact stood as USA Today reported. it was not an issue that as the GOP repeatedly screamed, had "poisoned" democracy in the 2020 presidential election.

USA Today was hardly the first journalist organization that set its near-divine mission to shine a light on the truth about alleged vote fraud in the nation. The GOP had been beating that drum for at least a decade before it exploded as Trump and the GOP's *cause celebre* in 2020. No place was it more of a clashing issue of contention than Florida.

* * * * *

In 2014, a defiant Florida GOP governor Rick Scott essentially told the Justice Department where it could go when it demanded that Florida stop its trumpeted campaign to purge tens of thousands of persons it claimed weren't eligible to vote. Despite Scott's bellicose rant against the Justice Department mandate, election officials in all Florida counties halted the purge effort.

Meanwhile, GOP state officials busily tried to figure out a way to end around the order to halt the voter purge. There was, of course, absolutely no proof of any widespread voting fraud. The overwhelming majority of those who Florida vote officials said were suspect was, of course, Black, and Hispanic voters. In many cases, they had taken painstaking steps to prove their citizenship.

Florida official's claim of massive potential vote fraud looked even more suspect when Miami-Dade County election officials sent out more than 1,500 warning letters and found a total of 13 people who said they were not citizens. Out of that gargantuan number they found that an even more stunning total of two persons that weren't citizens said they cast votes in the 1996 and 2000 and 2004 elections.

The underwhelming instances of fraud uncovered in Florida were no aberration. Studies that examined alleged voter fraud in Ohio and Wisconsin in the 2002 and 2004 elections found only a handful of actual cases of voter fraud. More than nine million votes were cast in the two states in both elections. Fast forward, nearly two decades later and the GOP was still using the same worn template virtually unchanged to allegedly prove that thousands illegally voted—all, of course, Black, and Hispanic, and all, of course, for the Democrats.

The GOP's bogus war on voter fraud then, and in the years after the Florida GOP vote fraud scam, was not about ensuring clean and fair elections, nabbing vote fraud lawbreakers, or upholding constitutional precepts. It's always been about winning elections on the cheap. It can only do that by tipping the vote number balance toward having more likely GOP voters and fewer likely Democratic voters. It's hardly a coincidence that the majority of those targeted for voter purges are Black and Hispanic.

It's even less of a coincidence that the bogus vote purge campaigns always zero in on the key battleground states of Florida, Ohio, Wisconsin, Pennsylvania, Texas, and

Arizona where election officials have relentlessly mounted similar purge campaigns.

The GOP re-learned a lesson from the 2000, 2004, 2008, and 2012 presidential elections. This was that numbers do count in close elections. And in the must-win states that determine who wins or loses the race to the White House, the smallest reduction in the number of Democratic voters can have a huge impact in determining the outcome of a close race. The numbers equation worked for the GOP in 2000 and 2004 and worked against it in 2008, and 2012 when Ohio, Colorado Wisconsin, and Florida switched party hands to the Democrats and did much to put President Obama in the White House.

Because of that, the GOP with a generous helping hand from the Supreme Court which upheld Indiana's stringent photo ID requirement in April 2008 then swung its voter fraud campaign into high gear.

It standardized a series of vote suppression mechanisms. They include:
- Making sure there is an absence of polling places in minority neighborhoods
- Claiming ballot and vote machine irregularities, using lists of foreclosed homes to challenge voter's residences
- Applying rigid timelines for filing voter applications
- Claiming the lack of information, misinformation, or deliberate disinformation about voter registration forms and materials

- Eliminating weekend voting, or sharply narrowing down the hours when polling places are open.

Estimates put the number of possibly eligible voters that are affected by the rash of new requirements when fully enforced at more than 20 million.

Obama also got a huge election shot in the arm from students and other youthful voters in 2008 and 2012. To counter that, several states moved quickly and prohibited the use of student IDs as voter eligible proof. In Wisconsin, students now must have a new student ID with a two-year expiration date to be eligible. In Virginia, the Republican-controlled State Board of Elections proposed tightening rules that make it easier for election officials to disqualify absentee ballots for even the most trivial mistake such as a misspelling on a signature.

GOP officials have not scrapped the old tried and true methods of voter suppression. They include district gerrymandering, tightening felon bans, skimping on the number of polling places and machines in mostly Black and Latino neighborhoods, stationing police at the polls, and challenging citizenship papers where they can get away with it. They will continue to plot against the 1965 Voting Rights Act long before its final 25-year renewal expiration date in 2032.

The GOP's bogus war on alleged voter fraud has been a stunning PR success in that it has convinced millions of Americans that massive numbers of mostly Blacks and Hispanics with the connivance of Democrats are knowingly breaking the law to vote against the GOP—when it's just the opposite. The Democrats scream foul at these thinly disguised suppression ploys, and mount court and Justice Department challenges, and a proposed sweeping voter protection law HR 1. The White House, Congress, and American democracy hang in the balance in the fight against the GOP's non-stop vote suppression schemes.

CHAPTER 3

SHOW ME THE MONEY AND THE CONSTITUTION

How much money do you have and how well do you know the Constitution? From 1877 until the late 1950s to the mid-1960s if you lived in Florida, Alabama, Tennessee, Arkansas, Louisiana, Mississippi, Georgia, North and South Carolina, Virginia, or Texas you had better have the cash and be a constitutional scholar to vote.

If you were deemed an eligible voter in those states, you had to shell out anywhere from $1.50 to $2.00 not to vote but to register to vote Which was equivalent to about $20.00 bucks (in 2020) Now that seems like a pittance today. If you were a dirt-poor farmer, sharecropper, day laborer, or more likely unemployed, in an era when there was no minimum wage, and wages were barely subsistence, that was a King's ransom. But remember the operative words were not vote but "register to vote."

Now, this is where the real fun began. In 1955 say, the poll tax-paying vote applicant, would stand in front of a local white vote registrar and write out in his/her handwriting (no assistance allowed) the answers to a barrage of 17 personal, intimate, and intrusive questions about themselves. If the applicant could somehow manage to wade through the questions satisfactorily, that was just the warm-up. The registrar would then require the applicant to answer these three questions.

18. WRITE AND COPY IN THE SPACE BELOW SECTION OF THE CONSTITUTION OF MISSISSIPPI [Instruction to the registrar: You will designate the section of the Constitution ~and point out same to applicant]:

19. WRITE IN THE SPACE BELOW A REASONABLE INTERPRETATION (THE MEANING) OF THE SECTION OF THE CONSTITUTION OF MISSISSIPPI WHICH YOU HAVE JUST COPIED:

20. WRITE IN THE SPACE BELOW A STATEMENT SETTING FORTH YOUR UNDERSTANDING OF THE DUTIES AND OBLIGATIONS OF CITIZENSHIP UNDER A CONSTITUTIONAL FORM OF GOVERNMENT.

A note, the Bold Capital letters were the brainchild of the Mississippi officials just in case anyone didn't get the message.

There was a similar variant of these constitutional stumping questions in Alabama, Georgia, and other deep South states.

* * * * *

Just how many of even the brightest constitutional scholars could answer those three questions to perfection was problematic, to say the least. However, these weren't constitutional scholars being asked the three questions. They were mostly poor Black voters. If the rarest of rare poor Black voter had the guts and temerity to show his or her face at the polling place, there was also the very real danger of violence and intimidation. The literacy test, the poll tax, and the threat of violence did exactly what it was supposed to do. That was totally exclude Blacks from the polls for nearly a century.

In pre-1960 Mississippi, there were more than two dozen counties where not a single Black was registered to vote. In other counties in the state, fewer than five percent of Blacks were registered. Mississippi was no aberration. Similar paltry Black registered vote totals were the norm in dozens of other counties in Georgia, Alabama, Louisiana, and North and South Carolina, less than five percent of Blacks were registered to vote.

The always interesting sidenote to the literacy tests and poll taxes was the hot denial by Southern white politicians that the literacy tests and taxes were racially skewed to bar Blacks from the polls. Southern legislators were careful never to put any racial stipulation on the tests and tax since whites supposedly had to pay the tax and take the same tests too.

But they didn't. They had a get out of tax and test card in the "Grandfather Clause." This permitted poor whites to vote if their grandfathers voted by 1867 or if they were the lineal descendants of voters back then. The clause did exactly what it was designed to do; namely make certain white men, even the poorest and dumbest white men, could vote without any hint that race had anything to do with it. It worked so well that of the more than 55,000 Blacks in Oklahoma in 1900, only 57 came from states that had permitted African Americans to vote in 1867.

The SCOTUS in a 1915 ruling ruled the grandfather clause unconstitutional. It made no difference. Some states simply turned around and grandfathered the grandfather clause with another time frame. Others, as usual in the South with any adverse federal court ruling on race, simply ignored it.

It would take the 1965 Voting Rights Act 1965 to do away with the insulting literacy tests. There was yet one more cruel racial insult to the systematic freeze out of Blacks from the polls. The 19th Amendment in 1920 gave women the right to vote, that is white women. Many Black women got a rude awakening when they turned up at the polls to vote after the amendment's passage. They found the polling door rudely slammed on them. Their gender didn't negate the racial requirement that they too had to pay a poll tax and pass the literacy test just like Black men.

Senator and former South Carolina Governor Benjamin Tillman was one of the prime architects of the near century-long airtight freeze out of millions of Blacks from the polls. On March 23, 1900, in a speech on the U.S. Senate floor, he brazenly and loudly bragged about why the South had to make sure Blacks never saw the inside of a voting booth:

"In my State, there were 135,000 negro voters, or negroes of voting age, and some 90,000 or 95,000 white voters... Now, I want to ask you, with a free vote and a fair count, how are you going to beat 135,000 by 95,000? How are you going to do it? You had set us an impossible task. The reason was about as straightforward plain as could be made." We of the South have never recognized the right of the negro to govern white men, and we never will...

At least Tillman was honest. Though he spoke a century and a quarter ago, his words still rang through the decades of pain, suffering, and violence that swirled around every effort, protest, march, demonstration mounted by civil rights groups against the Jim Crow voter exclusion of Blacks.

Tillman's crude but truthful words would be repeated in many variations and forms in the decades after President Lyndon Johnson on August 6, 1965, signed the Voting Rights Act. Since that moment, voter suppression has been embedded in the political fabric of the nation. The flowery promise in the 14th and 15th Amendments of equal protection under the law and the right to vote were measures that purportedly would confer in perpetuity the right of the newly freed slaves to the franchise. The promise has been little more than words on scraps of paper and ignored.

The language in the amendments was unambiguous, and the only real qualifier was the barrier for those convicted of felony crimes. This stipulation, though, opened wide the floodgate for disenfranchisement.

The South and a handful of other states wasted no time in latching unto this loophole. Three years after the passage of the amendments, nearly 30 states slapped bans on convicted felon voting. By the turn of the 20th century, only Maine and Vermont, two of the whitest states in the union, gave their residents the unrestricted right to vote.

"It is important to acknowledge that it has always, or almost for the entire history of our country, been about race," notes Sean Morales-Doyle, deputy director of Voting Rights and Elections at the Brennan Center," that voter suppression has been inextricably intertwined with an attempt to stop first Black men and since then other people of color from voting."

* * * * *

Another in the unsavory trilogy of voter suppression ploys that pre and post-dated the passage of the 1965 Voting Rights Act has been gerrymandering. Gerrymandering is simply weighting a district or carving out a district by redrawing the lines to ensure a majority of one race or one party in a district. In the South that almost always meant after the passage of the act crunching the numbers where Blacks outnumbered whites in an area and then moving that area to another district. It was not as crude and blatant a maneuver to preserve GOP political dominance as the vote suppression laws. But it provides a powerful disincentive for Blacks not to vote. At the very least it grossly dilutes the Black vote or Hispanic vote in gerrymandered districts.

"It's packing and cracking and you can use mathematical solutions to look at a state and look at where people of color are, especially Black people in a particular area distributed throughout the state," observes Christina Greer, an associate professor of Political Science at Fordham University. "And you can make districts where you can either pack them all into one or two districts."

The Brennan Center cited several districts both in the South and North where districts were deliberately redrawn to give one party a vote advantage over the other. While it's true that Democrats have done their own little gerrymander game to ensure Democratic-proof districts there is no evidence that it was done for the far more pernicious reason of ensuring a racially tainted vote advantage let alone dilute the Black or Hispanic vote. As has been proven, this is the case with the GOP.

* * * * *

The one man who benefited more than any other candidate in modern times from voter suppression, gerrymandering, and the history of voter exclusion was Trump in the 2016 presidential election. Numerous post-election surveys and studies confirmed that voter ID laws, putting the brakes on early voting, and slashing the number of voting places played right into his and the GOP's hands.

A study by the Atlantic and the Public Religion Research Institute found that one in ten Black and Hispanic respondents said either they were, or they knew of someone who was denied the vote because they did not have the "proper" identification or were listed incorrectly on the voter rolls. The figure for was whites was less than 5 percent. An even higher number of Blacks and Hispanics in the survey said they had trouble finding polling places on Election Day. A significant number were shut out because they missed the voting deadline. The figure for whites excluded from voting for those reasons was a fraction of that for Blacks and Hispanics in the super crucial battleground state of Wisconsin, as one example.

Voter ID restrictive roadblocks and the toss of ballots tilted the scale there to Trump. The single greatest plunge in votes from the 2012 election came in Black neighborhoods. The number who didn't vote because they lacked proper ID exceeded Trump's margin of victory in the battleground states. Some GOP officials even crowed that the tough voter ID restriction requirement put Trump over the top. They were right. Obama won Wisconsin twice in 2008 and 2012.

The big problem was the gaping perception among many persons that voting restrictive measures were a cause for worry. "Only 27 percent of white Americans say that eligible voters being denied the right to vote is a major problem today," notes Dan Cox, the research director at PRRI, and you have really strong majorities of black and Hispanic Americans—six in 10, roughly—saying that it is a major concern."

This lack of concern about the threat of restrictive measures plays directly into the GOP's hands. The last thing it wants is an aroused and enraged public demanding that the GOP cease and desist from its war on voting rights. One group that's certainly the case is corporations and business interest groups who serve as the willing paymasters for the GOP's vote suppression machinations.

CHAPTER 4

COLOR VOTE SUPPRESSION GREEN

In April 2020, nearly every major publication and news network headlined the story that America's corporate and financial biggies were up in arms over Georgia's very thinly disguised racially suppression law. On the surface, the checklist of major corporations that verbally opposed the law was impressive. The list included such corporate stalwarts as Coca-Cola, Delta, Black Rock, Merck. Porsche, Bank of America, Microsoft, Mercedes Benz, Citicorp JP Morgan, American Express, Viacom and Facebook, and Cisco. Even the flagrantly pro-Trump Home Depot top executives chimed in against it.

Nearly all the statements by the execs rang with the same theme, that voting rights are a sacred right that should be protected and open to all, that anything that hints of voter suppression is a bad thing and must be opposed. There was much talk about the law violating the spirit and letter of core corporate values. Pharmaceutical giant Merck said that the company stood "strong on our core values including our commitment to social justice and the right of people to fully and freely participate in electoral processes."

They all made ringing declarations that voting was the bedrock of a free society, "Brian Moynihan, chairman and CEO of Bank of America, told CNBC in a statement that, "The right to vote – and the vital work that must be done to protect access to that right – is a fundamental principle in the United States." "Our history in fact is punctuated by the moments," he further added, "when we expanded that right to those to whom it had been denied too long. We must continue to right the wrongs of our past and stand united in our advocacy for equal voting rights for all

Georgia Governor Brian Kemp quickly pushed back against the backlash of big money criticism. He lashed back that the criticism from business "ignores the content of the new law and unfortunately continues to spread the same false attacks being repeated by partisan activists."

Kemp even claimed that the law far from being so heinously restrictive expanded voting rights in dozens of Georgia counties by lengthening voting hours. What Kemp conveniently left out was that the bulk of those counties were a white majority, and top-heavy GOP leaning counties.

* * * * *

Kemp needn't have bothered haggling with the corporate executives over the right or wrong of the Georgia vote suppression law. There was little evidence beyond the corporate execs lofty words about upholding every American's unfettered right to vote without any barriers that they were taking any action to punish the Georgia GOP for passing the law. The Georgia vote law debacle was not the first time that major corporations flexed their muscle and spoke out against racial discrimination and injustice as being anathema to the American corporate way.

In the aftermath of the January 6, 2021, Capitol riot by the motley assortment of white nationalists, white supremacists, proud boys, neo-Nazis, and plain old Trump crazies, several corporate executives ripped the GOP for saying and doing nothing about the lawlessness. The news outlets went ecstatic over it. The newspapers and newscasts blazoned with headlines proclaiming that America's corporations were now strapping on their combat boots and going to battle against racial injustice.

That supposedly included calling out the GOP for its veiled racism. Some declared they'd publicly pledge to suspend their political action committee donations to Republican lawmakers who had tried to overturn the election.

This was the headline stuff. Behind the headlines, it was a far different story. The same corporations that were hailed as the defenders of the democratic realm were the same ones who routinely pumped millions into the two GOP groups that have been the most aggressive in filing lawsuits and court challenges to voting rights strengthening provisions and backing Trump's phony, silly, and frivolous bid to overturn the 2020 election.

The groups were the Republican State Leadership Committee and the Republican Attorneys General Association. Many of the same corporations were the leading lights in the U.S. Chamber of Commerce which has also battled hard against federal legislation protecting voting rights.

The corporations could hardly not know that the money they doled out to the Republican Attorneys General Association was used to fund anti-voting rights protections legal challenges. The association included Republican attorneys general from seventeen states: Alabama, Arkansas, Florida, Indiana, Kansas, Louisiana, Mississippi, Missouri, Montana, Nebraska, North Dakota, Oklahoma, South Carolina, South Dakota, Tennessee, Utah, and West Virginia.

Every one of these states was hardline Trump and GOP bastions. The corporate enablers that bankrolled voter suppression were not just the name-brand companies. More than forty companies and trade associations donated nearly $1.5 million to the Republican Attorneys General Association in December 2020 alone. All the while some of them were solemnly claiming they backed voting rights.

Here's one example of the double game the corporations play on voting rights. The Philadelphia-based international law firm Cozen O'Connor signed the "We Stand for Democracy" letter against voter suppression laws in April 2021. That was done in the front door for public consumption. In the back door, it shelled out $50,000 to the Republican AG group. The list of donors also included the better-known companies, Johnson & Johnson ($50,000), PepsiCo ($25,000), U.S. Sugar Corporation ($15,000), Microsoft ($25,000), Walmart ($125,000), and Blue Cross Blue Shield Association, ($15,000).

The Republican AGs have not been shy in taking corporate money and then turning right around filing voter law challenges and badgering and cajoling state legislatures to pass even more restrictive vote laws. The Biden win and the bare margin loss of the Senate and the House to the Democrats were tantamount to a declaration of political war by them. With a firm eye on the 2022 mid-term elections and a chance to grab back the House and the Senate, the AGs group is going full bore with challenge after challenge to decisively tip the skills in the GOP's favor with a multi-front voter suppression legal attack.

*****

Their tag team partner the Republican State Leadership Committee (RSLC), has been just as busy in the voter suppression battle. They have filed briefs with the Supreme Court demanding the court uphold Arizona's restrictive voter laws. This would be especially catastrophic since a decision in Arizona's favor would open wide the door to obliterate what's left of the enforcement provision of the Voting Rights Act.

The Committee's brief made just that point, "RSLC submits this brief in support of Petitioners because the Ninth Circuit's ruling if allowed to stand, will significantly undermine the ability of states to safeguard election integrity and maintain voter confidence, and will cause paralyzing uncertainty as to the continued validity of innumerable facially-neutral time, place, and manner election regulations."

The committee won't lack money to see that fight and others through. It got nearly $14 million from two hundred corporations and trade associations. It got the money after it filed its SCOTUS brief. The donors read like a who's who of the nation's top pharmaceuticals and health providers as well as other corporate bigshots. Health insurance giant, Centene Corporation contributed $250,000, while Anthem chipped in $50,000.

Pharmaceutical companies continued donating, too, including Novo Nordisk ($125,000), Novartis ($60,000), AbbVie ($50,000), and Gilead Sciences ($50,000).

Fossil fuel companies ExxonMobil and ConocoPhillips both gave $100,000 to the RSLC. Tech money poured in as well, including donations from Google ($25,000), Uber Technologies ($25,000), PayPal ($25,000), and Amazon ($10,000). Other corporate names, like Bank of America and Best Buy, each donated $25,000 to the RSLC. General Motors chipped in $10,000.

The committee plowed the money into an all-out campaign to encourage state legislatures to purge voter rolls, change voter registration deadlines, and enact new voter ID requirements. Liberal voting rights support groups have fought back, exposing the corporate massive donations to the right-wing vote suppression campaigns, and making public documents naming the companies and the amount of money they gave to these groups.

Accountable.US directly appealed to the companies to cease lending their name and dollars to the U.S. Chamber of Commerce and other vote suppression groups. The Chamber has been unmoved by the appeal. It quickly took the point in the fight against H.R. 1, the "For the People Act," that Biden and Congressional Democrats are pushing as the push back to the GOP's vote suppression ploys.

The one certainty, though, about the millions that corporations have funneled to the GOP groups. The same money will not be open to the Democratic and voter rights groups that vigorously oppose vote suppression.

CHAPTER 5

KICKING VOTE SUPPRESSION INTO HIGH GEAR

The fight to get more people to vote and the progress that has been made in expanding the voter rolls in the South and nationally after the Voting Rights Act was passed in 1965 almost came to a halt after the 2013 U.S. Supreme Court case, Shelby County v. Holder. The decision changed the way the Voting Rights Act was implemented nationwide.

In a 5-4 decision, Section 4 of the Voting Rights Act was ruled unconstitutional by the Supreme Court. According to the Department of Justice, "Section 4(a) of the Act established a formula to identify those areas and to provide for more stringent remedies where appropriate. The first of these targeted remedies was a five-year suspension of 'a test or device,' such as a literacy test as a prerequisite to register to vote."

The 2013 decision ruled that "the coverage formula set forth in Section 4(b) of the Act was unconstitutional, and consequently, no jurisdictions are now subject to the coverage formula in Section 4(b) or to Sections 4(f)(4) and 5 of Act. Accordingly, guidance information regarding the termination of coverage under Section 4(a) of the Voting Rights Act (i.e., bailout) from certain of the Act's special provisions is no longer necessary."

Chief Justice John Roberts, the longtime enemy of the Voting Rights Act, said the Voting Rights Act was based on the "decades-old data and eradicated practices ... such [literary] tests" and that they "have been banned nationwide for over 40 years. "While Jim Crow laws were banned nationwide because of the act, the floodgates were opened to allow states across the country to implement "massive dents" to the voting infrastructure in the United States, according to the Brennan Center.

Since 2010 before the decision, 25 states had put into place new requirements such as voter ID laws, closing polling places, and cutbacks to early voting, as per the Brennan Center. However, Texas and North Carolina faced challenges implementing these new laws.

In Texas, the state introduced a voter identification law to establish voter eligibility in its 2014 federal election, and while the move was ruled unconstitutional by U.S. District Judge Nelva Gonzales Ramos of Corpus Christi, the U.S. Supreme Court overruled the order.

In North Carolina, elected officials eliminated same-day registration, scaled back the early voting period, and implemented a photo identification requirement, however, U.S. District Judge Loretta Biggs issued an order barring the photo identification requirement. But as we stated, the SCOTUS stepped in and tossed the court's decision. The North Carolina legislature in subsequent years would pass even more restrictive voting laws.

* * * * *

"We are in the midst of what I think is a moment when American citizens and voters are taking voting rights and the way democracy works seriously and putting it at the top of their list of issues that they care about," Morales-Doyle said. "That's encouraging, and I hope it means that we'll take more steps forward in the near future."

These were indeed encouraging words, even fighting words in the voting rights wars. The brutal reality though was that the 2013 U.S. Supreme Court case, Shelby County v. Holder had two pernicious results. One, it changed the way the Voting Rights Act was implemented nationwide.

The second heart-rending consequence of the court's decision was that emboldened the GOP to skip the subterfuges and openly declare that their goal was indeed to suppress the vote, that is any vote against the GOP. Trump Senior campaign

advisor, Justin Clark noisily protested that his words had been taken badly out of context and baldly misunderstood when he was caught on a leaked audio in December 2019 telling a November 21 meeting of the Republican National Lawyers Association's Wisconsin chapter that "traditionally it's always been Republicans suppressing votes in places."

An annoyed Clark told the AP that what he meant was that he was just citing the litany of false accusations leveled at the GOP for according to him allegedly suppressing the vote.

That explanation might have flown at least for the GOP faithful. But then there was the other part of his statement that didn't sound exactly like an objective political history lesson. He implored the faithful to "Let's start protecting our voters Let's start playing offense a little bit. That's what you're going to see in 2020."

Clark had good reason to issue marching orders to GOP voters and officials in Wisconsin. Wisconsin along with Michigan and Pennsylvania were the must-win states Trump had to have to put him back in the White House. He won all three in 2016. Much depended in 2020 as in 2016, on the GOP getting as big a turnout as it could from GOP voters in those states. While at the same time getting as diminished a return as it could from traditional Democrats in those states. That invariably meant damping down the vote among Blacks, Hispanics, Youth, LGBT, and younger Asians in those states, especially in the bigger cities.

Clark wasn't the only kind of, sort of, honest guy among the GOP when it came to telling of their naked juggle of the laws to deliberately vote suppress in toss-up states. Texas was another case in point where a GOP official admitted what anyone who has ever watched the GOP manipulate the laws to boot potential Democrats from the polls knew.

Texas Attorney General Ken Paxton in a June 2021 podcast on white supremacists touting former Trump aide, Steve Bannon's media outlet didn't try to hide anything. He flatly admitted, almost bragged about it, that he blocked heavily

Democratic-leaning Harris County, with Houston its major city, from sending out mail-in ballots. Paxton crowed that if he hadn't done that then Biden may well have won Texas.

Paxton crunched the numbers to confirm his vote swindle, "Trump won by 620,000 votes in Texas,"(The) Harris County mail-in ballots that they wanted to send out were 2.5 million. Those were all illegal, and we were able to stop every one of them." Paxton offered zero evidence that the ballots were "illegal' which was impossible since they weren't ballots but ballot applications.

He did not exhibit the same even-handedness in blocking ballot applications from going out in rural counties in North Texas and Central Texas where the GOP dominates. Even if Paxton had not jerry-rigged the vote in Harris County, Biden still might not have won Texas. However, Paxton's frank admission of his role in derailing the process was yet another clear warning that more than a few GOP officials were brash enough to admit the obvious about their vote suppression ploys and dare anyone to do anything about it.

CHAPTER 6

"CONDITIONALLY SUSPECT"

THE NEVER-ENDING WAR AGAINST THE VOTING RIGHTS ACT

It was by no means a done deal. At least that was the deep concern of civil rights leaders as they accepted then-President Reagan's invitation to come to the White House on June 30, 1982, to witness his recertification of the 1965 Voting Rights Act. The provisions of the Act required congressional and presidential reapproval every 25 years to extend the provisions of the act.

The civil rights leaders were deeply concerned that Reagan given his virtual undeclared war with civil rights leaders over everything from opposition to affirmative action to the gutting of civil rights provision to his cozying up to GOP Southern ultra-conservatives might delay or even refuse to sign the Voting Rights Act extension. Reagan had once called the Act "humiliating to the South." As for signing the extension, he had said virtually nothing about his intention.

However, his Attorney General William French Smith had plenty to say about the extension. He strongly urged Reagan to take measures to weaken provisions of the Act. The main one being to let the South off the hook on the requirement that it get Justice Department approval for elections in areas that have had a dubious history of voter discrimination. Failing that, Smith urged Reagan to water down the Act. He didn't publicly at least specify what that meant. But the point was clear. Smith and other GOP conservatives close to Reagan weren't happy with the Voting Rights Act as it stood.

Reagan was having none of it. He signed the extension. However, Reagan gave a veiled warning, "Yes, there are differences over how to attain the equality we seek for all our people." NAACP president Benjamin Hooks caught the drift of Reagan's warning

and noted that he "belatedly" supported the measure and then added "I don't think it indicates any change of heart at all. The Justice Department has systematically rolled back enforcement of civil rights legislation."

It was an eerie Deja vu 25 years later on July 27, 2006, when then President Bush Jr. invited another coterie of civil rights leaders and congressional Democrats to the White House for his signing of the extension of the VRA. As with Reagan, there was some drama or rather pointed opposition to it. The same clique of Southern GOP conservatives and some Bush administration officials pulled the same page from the game plan they used with Reagan a quarter-century earlier and urged Bush not to sign the extension or demand some "modification" of the Act. They used the by now standard argument that it was unnecessary and was punitive to the South. There was even the threat to delay or even block passage in Congress.

A core of House Republicans did follow through on their threat to stall renewal. For more than a week, they dragged their feet on the legislation and demanded that hearings be held. They used the same old argument that it punishes the South for past voting-discrimination sins. They also didn't like the idea of bilingual ballots.

Bush as with Reagan ignored them and signed off on the extension in the White House ceremony. But Bush and Reagan's signatures on the Act's extension did nothing to quiet the war hoops from conservatives to gut the Act if not outright scrap it.

* * * * *

Seven years later conservatives finally had their long-held fond dream. They had a conservative majority on the SCOTUS. Even better, the newly installed SCOTUS Chief Justice John Roberts in 2005 was the one jurist who had protested the longest against the VRA. During those decades, Roberts canonized every argument that packs of GOP vote fraud adherents would self-righteously repeat. The VRA was an antiquated, outdated measure that no longer served the purpose for which it was originally needed.

In 1981, Attorney General William French Smith didn't come up with the idea to advise Reagan to go slow on signing the VRA. The idea was the brainchild of one of his legal aides, then 26-year-old John Roberts.

In a memo to Smith, Roberts noted "Something must be done to educate the Senators on the seriousness of this problem." He was even more emphatic and branded the Act, constitutionally suspect. Even before Roberts began his assault on the Voting Rights Act, there were warning signs of trouble ahead. Some years earlier Nixon floated the idea of eliminating the preclearance provision which was the centerpiece of the Act that gave the Justice Department the right to intervene in elections deemed discriminatory.

It quickly died after an outcry from civil rights organizations. Yet that was just the opening knell for the assault. There were more court decisions in the early 1980s that gnawed away at the Act. In each case, the decisions raised the legal bar practically to the roof in now requiring the plaintiffs to prove that there was a "racially discriminatory motivation" in a suspect biased vote in an election before bringing a discrimination lawsuit or challenge.

Congressional Democrats at that point with a comfortable majority and still with a core of moderate Republicans in the House and Senate beat back the effort. They enacted an amendment that banned any voting practice that "resulted in a denial or abridgment of the right of any citizen of the United States to vote on account of race or color."

Enter Roberts, he blitzed the Reagan officials with more than twenty-five memos imploring Reagan to greenlight the Justice Department to fight passage of the amendment. The saving grace to keep the act intact in those years was the still lingering fear and sensitivity by Republicans to be branded as racist.

Edward Blum, a wealthy anti-civil rights activist who would go on to be the driving force behind the Supreme Court case that gutted preclearance in 2013, complained in a 2006 National Review article, "Republicans don't want to be branded as hostile to minorities, especially just months from an election."

In 2013, the SCOTUS agreed to hear the infamous federal lawsuit by Shelby County, Alabama that had quietly worked its way up through the appeals courts. The county wanted much of the Act dumped and recycled the same old arguments that it is outdated, discriminatory, and a blatant federal intrusion into state's rights. In times past, this claim would have gone nowhere.

But 2013 was different. The SCOTUS now had a conservative majority. Meanwhile, attorneys general in several states endorsed the Alabama county's challenge. And when then-Attorney General Eric Holder announced that he'd vigorously enforce all provisions of the Voting Rights Act to prevent voter suppression, that ignited more fury from the GOP. The predictable happened. The SCOTUS struck down the provision that especially riled the GOP. The provision mandates prior federal approval of changes to voting procedures in parts of the country with a history of racial and other discrimination.

The parts were the South and the Southwest. The heavy-handed discrimination targets were Black and Hispanic voters whose numbers were growing. The result of those growing numbers was that states in the South and Southwest that had long been locked in the GOP vote column were now from the GOP's standpoint in danger of flipping to the Democrats.

* * * * *

As originally enacted, the Voting Rights Act required jurisdictions with a history of racist voting discrimination to "preclear" any new voting-related laws with the Justice Department or with federal judges in Washington, DC. But this preclearance provision was initially scheduled to expire five years after the law was signed in 1965.

That meant that in 1970, while Richard Nixon was president, Congress had to decide whether to extend the preclearance requirement or allow it to expire. And, because Congress never made the preclearance requirement permanent, Congress also chose to extend this requirement again in 1975, in 1982, and 2006. The GOP as is known undermined the Act with the rash of photo identification laws that the GOP governors and GOP controlled state legislatures enacted. They had one aim, and that was to discourage and ram down the number of minority and poor voters that overwhelmingly vote Democratic.

Despite the solid bipartisan support that the Act got in prior congresses and from GOP presidents, the Act has always been more controversial than many have believed. The popular myth is that congressional leaders were so appalled and enraged at the shocking TV clips of Alabama state troopers battering civil rights marchers in Selma in April 1965 that they promptly passed the landmark law that restored voting rights to Southern Blacks. What's forgotten is that the marchers were there in the first place because the bill was badly stalled in the Senate and the House. It took nearly five months to get the bill passed.

Then Senate minority leader, Illinois Republican Everett Dirksen, heaped amendments on the bill that included scrapping the poll tax ban, adding exemptions and escape clauses for Southern counties, and excluding all states outside the South. House Republicans tacked more amendments on the bill to weaken it. The fight over these amendments dragged on for weeks in Congress.

Now decades after that battle the danger that the SCOTUS will further gut the Act is real. The other grave danger is the couple of hundred voter suppression laws proposed in dozens of states, the GOP may get its long-standing goal. That's nothing less than a final burial of the Voting Rights Act. Their win would be democracy's loss. That was the grim reality the second year after Obama was reelected in 2012.

Three years after, Chief Justice SCOTUS Roberts was now in the legal driver's seat and could see to that. Given his avowed long history of antipathy to the Act, he left the heavy lifting to SCOTUS ultra-conservative Antonin Scalia during the court's oral arguments in Shelby County v. Holder (2013). He didn't disappoint, "I don't think there is anything to be gained by any Senator to vote against continuation of this act," Scalia continued. "And I am fairly confident it will be reenacted in perpetuity unless—unless a court can say it does not comport with the Constitution."

The court decision wiping out the hated by the white South and GOP conservative's preclearance provision was the crowning moment for Roberts. This proved his longtime argument that America had long since outgrown the dark days of Jim Crow exclusion of Blacks and had long since entered a new age of racial egalitarianism. The proof of that was the thousands of Black and Hispanic elected officials up to and including an African American president.

Roberts loftily declared". Yet nearly a half-century after the Voting Rights Act first became law, "the conditions that originally justified these measures no longer characterize voting in the covered jurisdictions." Black voter turnout "has come to exceed white voter turnout in five of the six states originally covered by" Section 5.

Robert's myopic, rosy view of a supposed color-blind America did not go unchallenged on the bench. Ruth Bader

Ginsburg in her dissenting opinion noted: "Throwing out preclearance when it has worked and is continuing to work to stop discriminatory changes is like throwing away your umbrella in a rainstorm because you are not getting wet."

The problem with all this was that even in the most horrific days of the Jim Crow racial freeze out of Blacks in the South, there was never a word in any of the laws, ordinances, legal tracts, or court rulings that mentioned race let along Blacks or Hispanics as being the explicit target of the vote freeze out. The exclusion was formalized through hints, nods, and legal subterfuges.

However, the result was the same. No Blacks voted even without the law saying that they couldn't. Some legislatures immediately took the hint from the 2013 court decision and with warp speed piled on various voter suppression restrictive laws –again always careful never to mention race. On the surface, the laws appeared to be completely race-neutral.

A near textbook example of this con game was the much-contested North Carolina vote law the GOP controlled legislature, quickly rushed through after the high court decision. Its voter ID requirement only permitted voters to use "those types of photo ID disproportionately held by whites and excluded those disproportionately held by African Americans." As one expert witness testified, several forms of ID that could not be used to vote under the North Carolina law—including government employee IDs, public assistance IDs, and student IDs—"provide relatively greater access to IDs for African Americans.

It was no accident that the states such as North Carolina were in the front ranks of those trying to take full advantage of the High Court's slash of the VRA. They are swing states and Black voters increasingly play a major role in breaking the GOP stranglehold on state, local and congressional offices in those states. Ratcheting down the number of Black voters in these states strikes a major blow to Democrat's effort to grab more state and federal offices. This would shift the political power equation. No surprise, though that when a federal appeals court struck down the North Carolina voting law, the Roberts High Court quickly upheld the law.

Roberts will not be satisfied until the Act is history. In one of his avalanche of earlier memos hammering the Act, he noted, "The Supreme Court has made clear that intent in this area ... may be proved by both direct and circumstantial evidence." The young Roberts wrote. Voting rights plaintiffs, "can rely on the historical background of official actions, departures from normal practice, and other indirect evidence in proving intent."

This is always the key conservative fallback argument, namely, prove intent. To prove any discrimination no matter how outlandish and evident simply producing numbers, charts, and the visible effect of the discrimination will never be enough. Short of getting into the head and minds of those who racially discriminate and prove they deliberately and knowingly "intended" to discriminate, it's a near impossibility to prove intent legally. This is the legal fiction and absurdity that Roberts operates under and when a voting discrimination case comes before his court that will be the ceiling-high bar he'll demand.

The GOP-controlled legislature and GOP governors have been emboldened by Robert's High Court to enact their rash of voter restrictive laws. They're secure in the knowledge that even when a federal appeals court strikes the restrictive laws down, they have a near-fail safe backstop in the Roberts High Court. The protective shield applies even when there are towering questions about how the ballots are counted in an election.

There's more. The Court's Republican majority, in an unsigned opinion joined by Roberts, held that many ballots in which there's any question of an irregularity must be trashed. The crux of the Court's decision in Republican National Committee v. Democratic National Committee (2020) was that it is more important to prevent courts from altering "the election rules on the eve of an election" than it is to ensure that every vote is counted. It makes absolutely no difference that tossing these ballots disenfranchises thousands of voters. It takes little imagination to guess just who most of these disenfranchised voters are likely to be.

* * * * *

There was one thing that Robert and his SCOTUS conservative majority cohorts despite their best obstructionist efforts couldn't stop. That was the election of Democratic Joe Biden in 2020. Nor could they stop the election for the first time practically in living memory of two Democratic senators in a special election in January 2021 in what had been for decades solid red state Georgia.

Their win gave Biden a paper-thin majority in the Senate. The election, though, was the red flag for the GOP. The shock of losing the state to Biden and then followed by the even greater shock of losing two GOP-held Senate seats in the run-off race to Democrats was too much for the party to stomach.

When the Voting Rights Act again comes up for consideration by the SCOTUS, it will rule on the other provision of the Act which has also been a major sore point for the GOP. That's section 2. It permits legal challenges to racial discrimination in voting procedures. Almost certainly, the justices will have one eye on Georgia's GOP governor Brian Kemp and the GOP controlled state legislatures' blatant effort to shove the state permanently back in the red state column with its naked, unabashed Jim Crow style vote suppression ploy.

This was just the warmup for the GOP's main act. That's to once and for all erase from the books, the 1965 Voting Rights Act. Thus, fulfilling the long-held dream of John Roberts.

The instant, though, the Supreme Court gutted the Voting Rights Act by knocking out the key provision requiring Justice Department pre-clearance before a locale can alter or institute new voting procedures, the call went up for Congress to restore some version of this requirement.

Then-President Barack Obama and then-Attorney General Eric Holder quickly added their voices to that call. The chances of that happening are nil if the GOP has its way.

The Supreme Court ruling was a dream come true for the GOP. It accomplished in one fell swoop what GOP leaders for the past three decades have strongly hinted they wanted doing and that's to water down the landmark 1965 Voting Rights Act to the point of irrelevancy. It floated several trial balloons in Congress in 1981 and again in 2006. The Act came up for renewal both times. Presidents Ronald Reagan and George W. Bush

ignored the calls from GOP hardliners and even some of their advisers who wanted them to delay signing the renewal authorization.

* * * * *

The argument was that the Act continues to punish the South for its history of blatant voting discrimination. But that past, the GOP claims, is just that, the past, and the proof is the thousands of Black and Hispanic state and local elected officials from the South and Southwest and the millions of black and Hispanic voters that are on the rolls in those states. The Supreme Court bought this argument. The Court majority deliberately ignored two glaring facts.

One is the well-documented present-day sneaky ways that local registrars devise ploys to limit or eliminate minority voters. The other is the wave of voter suppression laws that GOP governors and GOP-controlled state legislatures plopped on the books during the past few years to shoo Black and Hispanic voters from the polls.

Even though Black and Hispanic voters did vote in big numbers in the 2012 election, in many districts they still had to stand in endless lines, have their IDs thoroughly scrutinized, had no bilingual ballots, found voting hours shortened, and had to file legal challenges in state and federal courts to get injunctions to stop the more onerous of the voter suppression laws from being enforced.

The GOP vote suppression ruses for the most part fell flat on their face in 2012 when Black and Hispanic voters ducked around the fresh barriers put up and jammed the polls in near-record numbers. They provided the numbers that insured President Obama's reelection by a comfortable margin.

Though the GOP managed to maintain its grip on the five Deep South states, and other Old Confederacy states in the 2012 presidential election, almost exclusively with the majority votes of white conservatives, the increased number of Blacks and Hispanics in the states poses a mortal threat to continued GOP dominance in those states. That is if there are no barriers propped up to their registering and voting.

This is exactly why the GOP relied heavily on the Supreme Court dumping the crucial provision in the Act that insured a fair voting process. GOP leaders also knew that once the conservative Court majority ruled in its favor that some Democrats in Congress would almost certainly move to make over the law.

One obvious way is to broaden out the pre-clearance provision to include other areas of the country that have had or could have potential voting restriction issues and then ensuring that those jurisdictions be targeted for mandatory Justice Department monitoring. This would remove from the table the GOP's ancient contention that the Act unfairly targeted the South and some sections of the Southwest. This would easily pass constitutional muster since it would not single anyone district, region, or state for restrictive monitoring or Justice Department litigation.

Even this practical remake of the disputed parts of the Act is anathema to the GOP. If proposed, GOP congressional leaders would dither, delay, and loudly squeal again that voter discrimination is non-existent. And that there is no need for adding another burdensome provision to the Voting Rights Act. This is exactly what the GOP House members, though in a minority in the House in 2021 did. Not one voted for HR 1 the bill that would restore and enhance voting rights protections.

The harsh reality is that five judges essentially nullified what two GOP presidents and Congress with overwhelming bipartisan support for the past near half-century have routinely done. That's to ensure the much fought for and prized Voting Rights Act stays in some form on the books to ensure that a fair, equitable, and democratic voting process remains the law of the land. The exact American process the GOP has spent decades subverting.

CHAPTER 7

BACK TO THE EDMUND PETTUS BRIDGE

The GOP plays on the apathy and disinterest among much of the public about the importance of the voting rights protections. It uses this widespread indifference to work with near impunity to try to torpedo voting rights. However, many Americans are not asleep at the wheel when it comes to opposing at every turn the GOP's mendacious vote suppression ploys. True, the 2013 U.S. Supreme Court case, Shelby County v. Holder did throw a huge legal monkey wrench in the continued widespread enforcement of voting rights laws.

Roberts punctuated the slow down by giving it a

plausible legal cover when he wrote in as part of the majority opinion, "Voting Rights Act was based on the "decades-old data and eradicated practices ... such [literary] tests" and that they "have been banned nationwide for over 40 years." This was simply a red herring argument since voter suppression laws had absolutely nothing to do with whether a person could recite every provision of a state Constitution backward and forwards as in the old days.

Civil rights and voting rights advocates quickly turned to the lower courts to staunch the tidal wave of restrictive laws GOP-controlled legislatures were rushing through. The first was the always popular suppression tool, a restrictive voter identification law to establish voter eligibility.

In 2014, Texas passed this law. It was stricken down. The next of the favored suppression tools was the elimination of same-day registration and narrowing down the time frame for early voting and of course a restrictive photo ID. It was stricken down. The Roberts SCOTUS again came to the rescue and overturned both decisions.

The quick intervention by the SCOTUS to squash any federal appellate court rejection of the voter suppression laws, all or in part, sent the strong signal that the

courts alone could not be relied on to beat back voter suppression laws. Only Congress had the power to do that. This presented a possibility and a pitfall. The possibility lay first in the House. The Democratic-controlled House could and did act. It passed the HR 1 named the John Lewis Act in honor of the former congressional and civil rights icon John

Lewis. Not one GOP House rep supported the measure.

This was the sure indicator of what to expect when the bill went to the divided Senate. Senate Minority Leader Mitch McConnell quickly made clear that no GOP senator would vote for the measure. It would take ten GOP senators to get it through assuming all the Democratic senators held ranks in support of it.

The GOP senators could take their marching orders from the ever-vigilant ultra-conservative think tank, the Heritage Foundation. It spelled out its position in "The Facts About H.R. 1: For the People Act of 2021." It ticked off the by now familiar litany of conservative hit points on voting rights. It would impose federal control over state elections, would "erode" election protocols and safeguards to ensure voter eligibility, and wipe away means to ensure the accuracy of voter registration rolls.

Senate Democrats would marshal their argument refuting each one of the points. That would not move the needle one space with the GOP. The ultimate fallback was to continue to make the case publicly that voter suppression was a colossal danger to the democratic right to vote. The battle would have to be fought within and without the courts, and in every area of public opinion. There would and could be no shortcuts in this colossal battle.

*****

The truth is that the GOP never excepted the 2020 election result. This was the prime reason that GOP-controlled state legislatures introduced an even greater tidal wave of bills in more than two dozen states aimed at making sure there is no repeat of the 2020 election. The bills are mostly a rehash of the by now all too familiar voter suppression stuff.

They include scrapping or severely limiting mail-in balloting, mandatory IDs, purging voter rolls of those who change addresses, eliminating ballot drop boxes, shortening days and hours for drop-in voting, and same-day balloting. There was even some talk of circling back on the cockamamie ploy by Trump's Postmaster General to eliminate neighborhood mailboxes.

To cover, their naked, blatant, and insulting attempt to hijack all future elections, GOP vote suppressors continue to spin the shop-worn lie that the bills are aimed at ensuring that elections are fair, equitable, and free of fraud. Trump, of course, virtually institutionalized the lie of voter fraud by Democrats. However, long before Trump emerged on the presidential scene, the GOP busily concocted every ploy it could come up with to permanently excise as many Blacks, Hispanics, youth, and gays from the polls as possible. The assault began virtually the instant, the 1965 Voting Rights Act was passed.

The Act ignited the explosion in the number of Black, Hispanic, Asian, women, and Native American voters and the election of thousands of their number to local state and federal offices. The jewel in the crown in the Act was the election in 2008 of former President Obama.

The dozens of GOP voter suppression bills have been

the GOP's answer to Obama's two wins and Biden's win. They want no future repeat of either. Let's step back in time to the start of the GOP's long-running angst about voting rights. It started in March 1965 on the Edmund Pettus Bridge in Selma. One week after Alabama state troopers bludgeoned civil rights demonstrators on the bridge outside Selma on March 7, 1965, a visibly shaken Lyndon Johnson called for and addressed a joint session of Congress.

His message was clear. His administration would pull out all stops to pass a voting rights bill which was the objective of the Selma marches. Five months later, the bill became the landmark 1965 Voting Rights Act.

In the fifty-plus years since the Selma march and the passage of the Act, a succession of GOP leaders, state legislators, girded by various federal court decisions, and the reflexive rightist four, and sometimes, five U.S. Supreme Court justices, waged relentless war on the Act. The deal in the initial passage of the Act was that it be renewed every 25 years.

When the Act came up for renewal in 1981, hardline ultraconservatives in the administration of then-President Reagan made loud threats to push Reagan to oppose its renewal. They were just that, idle threats. Reagan with no fanfare signed the renewal legislation. When the Act came up for renewal again in 2006, the threats to thwart the law, turned into a mini-movement in Congress to delay or even block passage. A pack of House Republicans stalled the legislation for more than a week and demanded that hearings be held.

The standard attack line has always been that it punishes the South for past voting-discrimination sins and that the thousands of black and Hispanic legislators in the South, Southwest, and West is supreme proof that the crude, naked race-based voter suppression ploys were a thing of a long gone past. Bush signed the renewal order. But the GOP had served notice that the early saber rattle against the Act was just a warm-up for a full-throttle frontal assault.

The GOP burrowed away at eroding the Act with the rash of photo identification laws that the GOP governors and GOP controlled state legislatures enacted in recent years. The aim was to discourage and damp down the number of minority and poor voters that overwhelmingly vote Democratic.

GOP-controlled legislatures in six states in the South and Southwest where voting rights procedures were covered by that part of the act wasted no time in passing a slew of restrictive voting laws that the VRA had previously blocked. This brought the total to more than 20 states that have passed tough voting restrictions, according to the Brennan Center for Justice. This was only part of the story of the roadblocks the GOP has thrown up.

A study by the Alliance for Justice, a Washington D.C.-based, public interest group, documented legions of complaints and challenges filed by the Justice Department and voting rights groups to discriminatory changes that county registrars have made to eliminate or narrow down the number of voters in predominantly minority districts.

The tales of supposed massive voter fraud egged on by civil rights, voter rights advocacy groups, and supposedly orchestrated by the Democrats have been just that, self-serving tales. There is no evidence to support any of the GOP charges of massive voter hanky-panky.

Fifty years after the bloody Selma march shocked Johnson and the nation into taking fast track action to right a glaring historic wrong, namely the denial of the right to vote to millions in America, that right is still under intense assault. Therefore, we still need a Selma today.

CHAPTER 8

PLOTTING TO TAKE BACK THE WHITE HOUSE AND MUCH MORE

The GOP's relentless war on alleged rampant voter fraud targets, not thousands, as many critics have noted, but millions of eligible voters. To no surprise, the Brennan Center for Justice found that the majority of the five million eligible voters that could be banned from the polls under the new restrictive laws rammed into place in a dozen states by GOP governors and GOP controlled state legislatures were Black, Latino, or American Indian, low income, and young.

In 2008, these voters provided the decisive margin for President Obama's White House victory in Ohio, Pennsylvania, North Carolina, Florida, Virginia, and Colorado. In 2000 and 2004, Bush won five of these six states. In every case, he needed a solid turnout from older, white, conservative, overwhelmingly male voters to win.

That changed radically in 2008 with Obama's win. GOP strategists were determined that there would be no repeat of this in 2012 and unleashed their voter suppression campaign. Attorney General Eric Holder counter-attacked with Justice Department lawsuits, court actions, and injunctions to try to halt the GOP effort to suppress the vote.

Holder's fight back against the GOP's ham-fisted efforts to shoo as many poor, minority, and young voters away from the polls in November and beyond almost certainly is a major reason for the GOP's furious political mauling of him. GOP-controlled House committees launched investigation after investigation into Holder for everything from alleged perjury to malfeasance of office during his Justice Department tenure.

For the GOP, its voter suppression smokescreen was about numbers; two numbers to be exact. One number is the popular vote. Democratic presidential candidate Al Gore got a bigger share of the popular vote than Bush in 2000. He got that because of the heavy turnout in key states of the GOP's prime vote suppression targets, blacks, Latinos, and the young voters. In a super tight 2012 race, the five million voters that the Brennan Center documented as potential victims of the GOP's disenfranchising rash of voter ID and registration laws, could have tipped the popular vote to GOP presidential contender Mitt Romney.

The five million vote estimate turned out to be an undercount since some estimates put the number at more than 20 million possible eligible voters that potentially are affected by the torrent of GOP-driven requirements.

Gore's popular vote win in the presidential contest in 2000 showed a popular vote majority is meaningless without securing the 270 electoral votes needed to win the presidency. This is the second number the GOP's voter suppression campaign aims to attain. The states that have clamped on the new voter restrictions would consistently provide 171 electoral votes in presidential elections.

That's more than sixty percent of the total needed for a presidential candidate to bag the White House. The one crucial state that Obama did wrest from the GOP in 2008 and 2012, Pennsylvania, has been a special target of the GOP's suppression war. If the state's new stricter, voter ID law had been in place in both years, the margin of Obama's victory in the state would have been much smaller, if at all.

In 2016, the vote suppression campaign bore fruit for Trump. Who won both the popular vote and the state's electoral votes? He won because of a marked downtown in the Black and Hispanic votes in the state's urban areas.

The GOP claims that its only concern is to ensure clean and fair elections, nabbing vote fraud lawbreakers and upholding constitutional precepts of rampant voter fraud.

These are phony, self-serving fraudulent excuses. The rabidly partisan Republican National Lawyers' report in 2010 found a total of 400 election fraud prosecutions over a decade nationally. That's less than one per year per state. The underwhelming instance of fraud uncovered in Florida, which has drawn much public attention, is no aberration.

Studies that examined alleged voter fraud in Ohio and Wisconsin in the 2002 and 2004 elections found only a handful of actual cases of voter fraud. More than nine million votes were cast in the two states in both elections. That as has been shown was the same in the 2016 and 2020 presidential elections.

Holder made his most dogged challenge to the GOP voter suppression campaign in Texas which had enacted a rigid voter ID law. He bluntly called it a new poll tax, which is the racist weapon Southern states used for decades to keep Blacks from the polls. It took decades of protests, marches, litigation, and a Supreme Court decision to finally dump the poll tax.

The GOP hoped that its new voter suppression tactics would also hold up for years and through many elections to come, starting with the 2016 presidential election. It did that year. It didn't in 2020. However, the GOP is dead set that there be no repeat of 2020 in the coming presidential elections.

CHAPTER 9

THE FELON VOTING BAN IS A BLACK BAN

SEC. 1404. NOTIFICATION OF RESTORATION OF VOTING RIGHTS.

(a) State NOTIFICATION. —

(1) NOTIFICATION.—On the date determined under paragraph (2), each State shall notify in writing any individual who has been convicted of a criminal offense under the law of that State that such individual has the right to vote in an election for Federal office under the Democracy Restoration Act of 2019 and may register to vote in any such election and provide such individual with any materials that are necessary to register to vote in any such election.

This is one of the provisions in HR1 that the GOP most fears if the bill were ever to pass. The fear was first raised during the 2004 presidential campaign by then-Democratic presidential candidate John Kerry. He mildly protested the towering hurdles to ex-felon voting in dozens of states. Kerry raised the issue for a good reason. He was trying to unseat Republican incumbent President George Bush. He remembered what happened with the last Democratic candidate, Al Gore, in the 2000 presidential contest. Gore disputedly and arguably lost Florida to Bush by a few hundred votes. That cost him the White House.

A decade later, then-Attorney General Holder was diplomatic when he said that the time to end the full or partial bans in all but two states on ex-felons voting had long passed. The bans are a little short of medieval and disgraceful at best and at worst. The states that keep the bans on their books give real meaning to the term second-class citizenship for the millions of ex-felons who are barred from the polls or must go through tortuous loops to get their voting right restored. To no surprise, the disproportionate number of these felons is African American, and Holder said so.

Those few hundred votes almost certainly could have been easily swamped by thousands of Democratic votes in the state. A big portion of those Democratic votes would have come from Black voters. But thousands of those Black voters weren't there because they were permanently banned from the polls. They were among the thousands of ex-felons that Florida barred from the polls for life.

It made absolutely no difference whether the ex-felon

was imprisoned for petty drug use or murder. If it was a felony conviction, they were out. A handful could and did appeal to the Governor and some of the lucky ones did win their appeal to have the permanent ban lifted.

However, the loops they were forced to go through were tortuous, totally arbitrary, and humiliating. Nearly two decades later, Florida was back in the news again with a voter initiative, Voting Restoration Amendment, to lift the ex-felon voting lifetime ban. It passed. However, the GOP-controlled legislature and Florida's GOP governor rushed into action and passed a series of bills that would in effect water down the effect of the Act.

The measure mandated that anyone with a felony record that sought vote reinstatement had to shell out money to pay any financial obligation they had from their sentencing or get a judge to waive them before being allowed to vote. This was a giant hurdle for many low-income and indigent former felons. That was the idea. The last thing the GOP in the state wanted was packs of Black and Hispanic ex-felons trudging to the polls and punching the Democratic party ticket.

*****

The Florida ex-felon vote ban had nothing to do with protecting society, preserving order, or punishment. It had everything to do with politics and race. They can't be separated. It's no coincidence that the states that impose the medieval lifetime or close to lifetime bans on ex-felons, like Florida, are mostly Deep South states.

In a speech at Georgetown University in February 2014, Holder was diplomatic when he said that the time to end the full or partial bans in all but two states on ex-felons voting had long passed. What Holder didn't say is that these are the men and women who in decades past were victims of racist poll taxes, literacy laws, and political gerrymandering.

They were driven from the voting booths by physical harassment, threats, and intimidation by bigoted sheriffs and voter registrars. As heinous and deplorable as that was, it at least made some perverse sense only because blatant Jim Crow racist vote disenfranchisement had clear political intent and that was to preserve white political power in and outside the South. That intent almost certainly was still very much a factor in the political calculus of the GOP in the immediate decades after the collapse of legal segregation.

To be even blunter, the bans are a 21st Century update of the old Jim Crow disenfranchisement ploys the South has used for decades to dilute the Black vote. The arsenal of racially abusive tactics has included poll taxes, literacy laws, and political gerrymandering to drive Blacks from the voting booths. The states are all GOP-controlled. The resistance from the GOP governors and state legislatures to modifying, let alone scrapping the harsh bans, has been fierce.

This thinly disguised relic of the South's Jim Crow past also has done much to drastically dilute Black political strength. In the 2016 presidential election, if the 1 million Black men in prison, on parole, or probation that was disenfranchised because of their criminal record had been added to the total their vote might have made a crucial difference in putting Hillary Clinton not Trump in the White House as well as other close statewide contests.

Black ex-felon disenfranchisement will probably get worse. Blacks still make up nearly half of the more than 2 million prisoners in the nation's jails. The continued entrenchment of racially biased drug laws, racial profiling, and chronic poverty in many Black communities means that more Black men will be arrested, prosecuted, convicted, and serve longer prison sentences than white men. This virtually guarantees that the number of Blacks behind bars will continue to be higher than any other ethnic group in America.

The Sentencing Project in its yearly reports estimates that at the present rate of Black incarceration upwards of 40 percent of black men could be permanently barred from the polls in the vote-restricted states in the next few years. Many conservatives passionately defend the policy of ex-felon disenfranchisement. They claim that in barring criminals from voting society sends the strong message that if you break the law, you should pay and continue to pay dearly. The argument might make sense if all or most of the disenfranchised ex-felons were convicted murderers, rapists, or robbers. And they were denied the vote because of a court-imposed sentence.

This is not the case. None of the states that bar felons from voting in near perpetuity require that judges strip them of their voting rights as part of their sentence based on the seriousness of the crime or the severity of the punishment. Most ex-felons are jailed for non-violent crimes such as drug possession, passing bad checks, or auto theft.

In most instances, they fully served their sentence and in theory, paid their debt to society. Most of the convicted felons were young men when they committed their crimes. The odds are that most of them won't become career criminals, but will hold steady jobs, raise families, and become responsible members of the community.

Yet imprinting these ex-felons with the legal and social stigma of "hereditary criminals" and banning them from voting until death makes politicians and many Americans seem like the worst kind of hypocrites when they say they believe in giving prisoners a second chance in life. Civil liberties groups and civil rights organizations must fight harder against the bans. That means filing court challenges and mounting a sustained lobbying campaign in Congress or state legislatures to get the discriminatory voting laws changed.

The denial of voting rights to thousands of Blacks, decades after the end of slavery and legal segregation is a travesty of justice and a blot on the democratic process. If Florida GOP officials, as well as those in other states, and the GOP continue to have their way the travesty will continue.

Let's return to Holder's call for scrapping the felon voting ban in his 2014 Georgetown speech. He had barely finished his call to the states to dump the felon voting bans than Republican governors in Iowa and Florida made it clear that they did not see the felon bans as racially biased, and a blight on society and that they had no intention of touching the laws.

It's worth noting that Holder's call then for an end to the bans was just that a call. The attorney general had no authority to compel the states to act on the bans. Worse, there have been few court challenges from civil liberties organizations that have been completely successful. Despite the slightly shifting tide in public opinion about drug laws, sentencing, and even a rethink of treatment and rehabilitation for non-violent offenders, few public officials are willing to be cursed as "soft on crime," and most state legislatures have ignored the issue. A bill, for instance, once touted by former Michigan Democrat John Conyers over the years to lift the prohibition on ex-felon voting never got any traction in Congress.

The only way ex-felons can get their voting rights restored is to seek a pardon from the governor. However, this is a dead-end for most as Florida certainly showed. So, few ex-felons still even bother to request a pardon.

In 2014, Holder did the right thing by attempting to verbally whipsaw the states to play fair with ex-felons and end their disenfranchisement. But for all his good intentions, the fight to end the nation's disgraceful ex-felon vote bans years after his call is a tough sled precisely because it remains one of the GOP's greatest and most effective voter suppression weapons.

CHAPTER 10

THE GRAVE DANGER TO DEMOCRATS IN 2022

In March 2021, New Jersey Democratic Senator Corey Booker flatly called the Georgia gubernatorial election a theft for GOP winner Brian Kemp. This was not partisan hyperbole. Thousands of eligible votes weren't registered, were tossed, discounted, or ignored. The process was only slightly less muddled and outrageous in Florida where there were also widespread reports of irregularities, incompetence, fraud, and manipulation.

The result in both states was that Democratic contender Stacey Abrams in Georgia and Andrew Gillum in Florida didn't make history by being the first Black governors in their states. Instead, they made history by being embroiled in rancor and controversy over the voting process. The brutal reality, though, was that no matter how many votes Gillum and Abrams got or would have gotten in a fair process where all the votes were allowed and counted, their defeat was almost pre-ordained before the first shout of voter fraud was made in their races.

Voter suppression is a well-documented fact of life in American politics. The GOP has welded it as a potent weapon to assure its continued domination of American politics. The even more terrifying reality is that vote suppression has the force of law behind it. Kemp in Georgia was the crudest example of that. As secretary of state, he could legally make the call about which votes could and couldn't be counted. The lawsuits that were filed against his blatant vote suppression were at best stop-gap efforts to blunt some of the damage. They did absolutely nothing to change the legal authority Kemp had to make the call about the voting process.

The vote suppression ploys the GOP employ in a variety of other stats include closing polling places, limiting voting hours, a rigid requirement for ID, and outright purging voters from the rolls if they haven't voted in a recent election. These were all upheld by various courts including the Supreme Court.

With few exceptions, the other GOP voter suppression ploy of tightly gerrymandering districts to make it impregnable to a Democratic contender has also been let stand in court challenges. This combined with the control of the voting process by GOP governors and GOP-controlled legislatures in Florida and Ohio, the two states that virtually determine who sits in the Oval Office, heightened the danger to Democrats in 2020.

* * * * *

The combination of a determined Democratic party ground game, an aroused Democratic voting base and greater turnout, and aggressive legal challenges to the GOP voter suppression tactics was enough to put Biden over the top in 2020. However, there is 2022, the mid-term elections. The full force of the GOP vote suppression laws could well be in full force by then, further imperiling the Democrats.

It's the legality of voter suppression that is the toughest nut to crack. Its impregnability was made possible by the GOP's crass, cynical, but stupendously successful assault on the landmark 1965 Voting Rights Act. The GOP twice got and won in two landmark decisions by the SCOTUS its stock characterization of the Act as outdated, discriminatory, and a blatant federal intrusion into state's rights. Each time the court gutted enforcement provisions of the Act, GOP states attorneys general in several states led the charge with briefs in support of doing away with the provisions.

The shock of the defeat of Trump in the 2020 presidential election far from being a point of discouragement, was a call to renewed battle for the GOP. It has kicked voter suppression into high gear with the rash of photo identification laws that the GOP governors and GOP-controlled state legislatures have enacted. The odious history of these laws badly discolored and even undergirded the GOP's vote suppression ploys that played a big part in Gillum and Abram's losses.

Congressional Democrats are very mindful of this history and thus the craft of HR 1, which is a series of democratic reforms to break the stifling grip of voter suppression hijinks. A centerpiece will be automatic voter registration which will automatically add eligible voters to the rolls. The GOP, of course, will use every legislative and parliamentary trick in its arsenal to ensure the voting rights reforms die a slow death. The agony of their stall, duck, dodge, and obstruct tactics will once more spotlight the grave danger that voter GOP suppression poses to the Democrats in 2022 and beyond.

CHAPTER 11

THEN THERE'S THE ELECTORAL COLLEGE

"The electoral college is a disaster for a democracy."
—Donald J. Trump (@realDonaldTrump)
November 7, 2012

Now just why would Trump tweet that in November 2012 about the Electoral College? The answer is simple. He was not running for president then. He had also not just won a presidency four years later by getting millions more popular votes than his rival Democratic presidential candidate Hillary Clinton. In fact, he broke a dubious record of sorts by being the winning presidential candidate with the fewest number of popular votes than any other winning popular vote losing president in American history.

No matter, he still grabbed the White House, and he did it courtesy of besting Clinton in the number of Electoral votes he got. So, there wasn't much of a surprise when Trump almost exactly four years later tweeted this: "The Electoral College is actually genius in that it brings all states, including the smaller ones, into play. Campaigning is much different!"

—Donald J. Trump (@realDonaldTrump)
November 15, 2016

Trump sang a different stanza on the worth of the Electoral College because he won with it. But the GOP had long since been a prime defender of the Electoral College. It fit squarely in with its relentless campaign to vote suppress by ensuring that GOP presidential candidates could virtually be assured of maintaining their lock on the six or seven states that in recent past elections have decided the White House winner.

The Trump win was a classic vindication of that GOP strategy. Trump won Michigan, Pennsylvania and Wisconsin, and North Carolina. They put him over the top. It was no accident that these were states where the GOP had worked overtime with lawsuits, legislation, and various maneuvers to damp down the Black and Hispanic vote.

Trump now had the dubious distinction of being the second GOP President to benefit from the combination of a watered-down Black and Hispanic vote that resulted in a win through the Electoral College. The other was George Bush Jr in 2000.

Let's fine-tune the GOP's huge advantage by welding voter suppression with the Electoral College. In the 2016 presidential election. Trump and rival Hillary Clinton made a combined 250 plus official campaign vote trips to Pennsylvania, Florida, North Carolina, Ohio, Michigan, and Wisconsin. This was exactly 250 plus more visits than they made to California and New York, the nation's most populist states, and the states with by far the largest number of Black, Hispanic and Asian voters.

Eighteen states got no visits from either of them. There was no need. Long before the first vote was cast, voters in the eighteen states and their Electoral College votes had already been earmarked for either Clinton or Trump. They were rock-solid, unshakeable either GOP or Democratic majority states that were safely in the candidate's respective bags.

* * * * *

The Electoral College, though, isn't the only reason national elections aren't national. And why a handful of states determine the national winner out of all proportion to their population and location.

Wisconsin and Michigan have a combined 36 electoral votes, while New York and California dwarf them with their massive number of electoral votes. Yet California and New York got a paltry two presidential visits, and both were from Clinton.

The six presidential maker states also have an

even-sized mix of Democrats, Republicans, and independents. However, that must be fine-tuned, and Trump showed how. He pitched a relatively small narrow base of voters in the suburbs and rural parts of the six states with his quasi-economic populist, full-throated race, and immigrant-bashing, America first, demagogic campaign. This was just enough to ensure that these voters stormed the polls and gave him the razor edge he needed to win several of these states.

Meanwhile, the GOP pulled out every trick from lawsuits to legislation to shove down the Black and Hispanic vote. This tact would not have worked if these voters were in any of the other states that were either reliably Democrat or Republican.

Trump tried to do the same in the 2020 presidential campaign. The difference this time was that his Democratic presidential rival, Biden, did the same by trying to peel off some of the Trump base but especially ramping up the vote among Blacks, Hispanics, young persons, and suburban college-educated women, to offset the Trump crowd. This was done clearly with an eye on ensuring a win in the Electoral College in the states that Trump won through the EC in 2016.

Biden and the Democrats were successful with this riveted-up vote strategy in the 2020 election. However, the problem with this is that it still gave outsized power to the handful of states and effectively marginalizes the other forty-four.

Then There's the Electoral College

* * * * *

This will continue to have dire consequences. It makes eligible voters even less inclined to make any effort to go to the polls. The thinking is what difference does it make, the game is already rigged, and my vote doesn't count. Appeals that there's more at stake in a presidential election than just the presidency, but that lots of local and state offices and ballot initiatives are just as important, and votes for them count to flop when the mass media and public fixate on the race to the White House.

This malaise hurts Democrats far more than Republicans because their voter base is far more diverse, eclectic, and with many younger voters, fickle. It's also the base that is the main target of GOP vote suppression tactics.

It's repeatedly said that it's outrageous that six states are the shot callers in a national election. This makes a mockery of the pretense that the popular vote is what elections should be about. If a less-educated white rural or blue-collar voter can get all the attention from Trump and even a Democratic presidential candidate, the message is that their vote in six states means everything, while a vote in the other forty-four states is means nothing. It also means that minority voters who the Democrats bank on to deliver wins for them in these states continue to be the most vulnerable to vote suppression.

This again points squarely to the problem of race. It's not that the handful of states that decide presidential elections are the whitest states in the union. That distinction goes to states such as Vermont or Idaho. Both states are either lock down GOP or Democratic states. It's the sometimes subtle, sometimes blatant, racial pandering to certain voters in the swing states that's the problem.

The hard reality is that the GOP could not have been competitive during the 2008, 2012 and the 2016 presidential campaigns without the bailout from rural, less educated, lower-income, white male, and female voters.

Six states, then, with larger numbers of these voters are the undisputed kingmakers in national politics. Toss in the stepped-up drive by the GOP in these key states to whittle down the number of Black and Hispanic voters that are deemed vote eligible, the Electoral College will almost certainly continue to be the reliable ace card for the GOP to win or at the least stay close to keeping its lock on the Oval Office.

CHAPTER 12

THE RACIAL VOTE SUPPRESSION CARD

It was an interesting moment in March 2013 at the National Press Club in Washington D.C. Then Republican National Committee chair Reince Priebus unveiled a hundred-plus-page blueprint on how to dispel the public's image of the GOP as a haven for unreconstructed bigots and professional Obama haters. A centerpiece of the campaign was the pledge to immediately blast anyone in or affiliated with the GOP who popped off with a hate rant about minorities or gays.

It was a tough sell for a bigger reason than just the need to smack down an individual bigot. So tough, that the pledge was forgotten almost as soon as it was made. In the years since the pledge, the GOP locals, chapters, and affiliated support groups have been honey-combed with individuals that have openly boasted of their white nationalist, proud boys, patriot, and ne0Nazi ties.

Now with Trump in the White House in 2016, that seemed to put the lie for good to the claim that the GOP had embarked on a wholesale purge of its ultra-conservative, even race-baiting legion of backers. The GOP's flat refusal to back any real congressional probe of the January 6, 2021, Capitol riot by the vast assortment of GOP affiliated racists and rightists was the crowning refutation of Priebus's long ago and long forgotten pledge to clean the stables GOP stables of racists. Even before Priebus pledged, a loud bell ring that a purge was the last thing the GOP wanted or could afford.

Priebus, though, was careful to note in his 100-point minority voter plan that it represented a bid for greater inclusion. But it in no way represented a fundamental policy change by the GOP.

On a cable talk show appearance in 2010, then-Senate Minority Leader Mitch McConnell flatly refused several direct, angled, and nuanced efforts to discuss racism in the tea party. McConnell's none too subtle refusal to weigh in on the issue was in direct response to the NAACP's resolution demanding that the Tea Party speak out, and speak out loudly against the racists among them.

Long before the NAACP stirred debate on tea party racism with its resolution, a legion of Democrats, civil rights leaders, and even an online petition from an advocacy group begged the GOP to speak out against its naked bigots. No go.

* * * * *

There was a good reason. That reason strikes to the heart of why the GOP has been so dogged and hidebound to nail any vestige of fair and equitable voting among Blacks and Hispanics in the states where their votes could end GOP political dominance. Put bluntly, the GOP cannot win a national election without the maximum number of white, rural, blue-collar lower-income, and educated white males and females.

The spark of playing on race to reignite the GOP's traditional conservative, white male loyalists, and increasingly white female supporters, has always been there. The 2008 and 2012 presidential elections gave ample warning of that. While Obama made a breakthrough in winning a significant percent of votes from white independents and young white voters, his GOP presidential opponents John McCain in 2008 and Mitt Romney (not Obama) in 2012 won a slim majority of their vote in the final tally.

Overall, Obama garnered slightly more than 40 percent of the white male vote. Among white male voters in the South and heartland, Obama made almost no impact. Overall, McCain and Romney garnered nearly 60 percent of the white vote.

The GOP could not have been competitive during the 2008 and 2012 campaigns without the bailout from white male voters. Much has been made since then that they are a dwindling percent of the electorate and that Hispanics, Asian, Black, young, and women voters will permanently tip the balance of political power to the Democrats in coming national elections. Blue-collar white voters have shrunk from more than half of the nation's voters to less than 40 percent.

The assumption, based solely on this slide and the increased minority population numbers and regional demographic changes, is that the GOP's white vote strategy is doomed to fail. This ignores three political facts. 1) Elections are usually won by candidates with a solid and impassioned core of bloc voters. 2) White males, particularly older white males, vote consistently and faithfully. And 3) they voted in a far greater percentage than Hispanics and Blacks.

* * * * *

GOP leaders and especially Trump have long known that blue-collar and a significant percentage of college-educated, white male voters, who are professionals can be easily aroused to vote and shout on the emotional wedge issues, abortion, family values, anti-gay marriage, and tax cuts. They whipped up their hysteria and borderline racism against the Affordable Care Act, and by extension Obama. This was glaringly apparent in the ferocity and bile spouted by the shock troops the GOP leaders in consort with the Tea Party activists brought out to harangue, harass and bully

Democrat legislators on the eve of the health care vote in 2009.

These were the very voters that GOP presidents and aspiring presidents, Nixon, Reagan, Bush Sr. and George W. Bush, McCain, and Romney, and above all, Trump, and an endless line of GOP governors, senators, and congresspersons have relied on for victory and to seize and maintain regional and national political dominance.

The GOP is widely seen, as an insular party of Deep South and narrow Heartland, rural and non-college-educated blue-collar whites. But this is not a voting demographic to mock, ridicule, or be sneered at, let alone dismiss because the numbers are still huge.

The GOP is driven by personal instinct, political leanings, its history, racial demographics, and raw political need, has masterfully played the race card for more than a half-century to get its way. Trump studied the template well and managed to add a few tweaks to it, with his swagger and bluster.

The political jewel in the crown, though, is and will remain voter suppression. This has been the time-tested ploy that has brought a big political pay-off for GOP candidates and incumbents from the lowest level of local offices to the White House. Asking the GOP to play fair with the American vote process would be asking the GOP to cut its own throat.

CHAPTER 13

OBAMA SHOWED THE WAY

Joe Biden, no not President Joe Biden, but then Vice president Joe Biden, unlocked one of the keys to combatting if not beating back the GOP's voter suppression ploys. It was a couple of days before the 2012 presidential election campaign, and Biden was campaigning in one of the must-win states, Colorado, a key swing state.

Biden was there to talk to the Obama campaign's boots on the ground volunteers. Biden was the picture of confidence win he told the volunteers that their "ground operation was the best in the history of presidential politics." It was over-the-top hyperbole by any count. What wasn't was his next statement. He specifically singled out Virginia and

Florida as the states that he said would most likely determine the election.

Both were key swing states with a lot of combined electoral votes. They were also states, especially Florida, that were perennial states that the GOP targeted with every ruse and ploy to damp down the Black and Hispanic, especially the young Hispanic, vote in Florida which was increasingly trending Democrat vote. In a close election, this would make the difference.

Biden understood that the election was in part a numbers game, and in greater part of a game of who could avoid the pitfalls of letting the opposition gain one-upmanship over the party with the vote numbers. The Obama campaign mixed several key components. It established a massive number of field offices, more campaign volunteers, lots of neighborhood team leaders, phone bank callers and volunteers, and lots of personal contacts with voters. They made two other key decisions. They focused the mass of their campaign armada in the handful of swing states that in the past had been GOP-protected preserves such as Ohio, New Hampshire, and Florida.

The second decision was to finely attune the campaign's antenna to any voter suppression ploy that the GOP would attempt and then be instantly prepared to challenge it. The campaign kept its sharpest eye on Black and Hispanic voters in those states who would be the most likely target of any vote suppression gambit.

* * * * *

It was essential to counter this by maintaining constant contact with and constantly motivating these voters to turn out on Election Day. Nothing could be left to chance, taken for granted, or assumed given the high stakes, and the proven capability of the GOP to vote suppress in urban neighborhoods.

The key though was to give Black and Hispanic voters a sense that the election meant much to them and could change their lives for the better.

There were early signs that it would be an uphill battle to convey that sense. A Pew Research Poll Center Poll in early May 2008 found that "inspiring," "fresh," "change," and "visionary" was not the word voters said best described Obama. The word was "inexperienced." Republican presidential contender John McCain has made this and the boast that he was the best on national security, the terrorist fight and defense preparedness his attack mantra against Obama.

Obama parried the attack by turning the table and proclaiming that his lack of national and especially international experience is a positive. That he'd bring fresh ideas and approaches to statecraft that replace the old, tired, and failed policies of recent times.

That was not enough. He had to choose a vice presidential running mate who was every bit the tough guy on national security, the war on terrorism, and defense preparedness that McCain claimed to be. Then he had to convince voters that he'd back up his pledge to bring an honorable and workable end to the Iraq war. He also could not rely solely on then President Bush Jr. and the GOP's domestic fumbles to do the job for him.

This brought the campaign back to the basics. That was to build a top-notch, high-energy ground game that could not just get out the Democratic vote but energize the Democratic voters. He started by making the ringing call by the Democrats for party unity more than a feel-good, politically correct self-assuring call. That meant repairing the deep polarization among Democratic voters, or more particularly, the hardliners who backed Hillary Clinton and were wary if not hostile to him.

He tried to convince white blue-collar and rural whites that an Obama White House would aggressively battle against soaring gas prices, home foreclosures, job losses, plant closures, the erosion of farm supports and to implement affordable health care and a McCain White House wouldn't. He had to make an equally all-out effort to convince Latinos that an Obama White House would just as aggressively fight for immigration reform and affordable health care, and a McCain or a Romney White House wouldn't.

The real key remained to turn his campaigns for the White House into a holy crusade among Black and Latino voters. The bellwether for that was Obama's smash victory in the South Carolina primary in January 2009. More than a half-million Democrats voted. That was near twice the

Democratic turnout of 2004 and almost 20 percent higher than the Republican vote the week before. Blacks made up more than half of the Democratic vote in the state. In California, Latinos made up nearly 30 percent of the voters.

Obama then really cranked the ground game up in the closing weeks before the elections in 2008 and 2012 He made sure that the near-record numbers that flooded the polls in the Democratic primaries flooded the polls in near-record or better yet record numbers in the fall election. He turned part of his campaign into a bully pulpit to speak out on the need for vigilance on and civil rights protections and especially voting rights protections. Even this was not a total guarantee of victory given the GOP efforts to place vote place barriers before minority voters. He needed extra insurance.

He found that by convincing the one bloc of voters that the GOP would never dare target for vote suppression. They were moderate to conservative white independent voters in the swing states. He convinced a significant number of them that he was the real change alternative in handling the war, the economy, health care, immigration, and energy issues.

It was the perfect storm—-change, moderation, hope, and most importantly, energizing Black and Hispanic voters that were often wary, discouraged, and cast out from the voting process through various legal dodges. By bringing all the right political elements together, Obama twice showed the way to forcefully combat even the most outrageous voter suppression roadblocks the GOP put in place then and now.

* * * * *

The template he set was put in play once more in Georgia in the 2020 presidential election. No Democratic presidential candidate had won the state since Jimmy Carter in 1976. He won mostly because he was a former Georgia governor, and a rock-solid Georgia native son. Biden broke the four decades plus GOP stranglehold on the presidential winner by updating the Obama playbook. The playbook master was former Georgia state legislator Stacey Abrams. She did five things that borrowed from and enhanced the Obama winning strategy.

She formed and was the driving force behind two explicit voter education, registration, and mobilization groups, New Georgia Project, and Fair Fight. She put waves of boots on the ground volunteers in the field, on phones, handling mailings and social media blasts, and contacts with registered voters. She heavily targeted young persons, college students, and multitudes of African Americans and Hispanics that were non-voters or bare sometimes voters.

She convinced the Democratic party organizations, labor unions, and religious groups to pour lots of cash into the grassroots boots-on-the-ground campaign. She

repeatedly lambasted and mounted legal challenges to Georgia's outlandish voter roll cleansing swipes of mostly Black and Hispanic eligible voters. She thought and planned long term.

The campaign was not just to flip Georgia for Biden

and elect two Democratic senators, but to build a permanent structure with teeth and body to win races at the local and state level future. A centerpiece of this long-term strategy would continue to be the ongoing battle against GOP voter suppression.

Obama first, then Abrams showed that even in the face of the most horrendous restrictive GOP vote suppression measures, democracy can still win out. It just takes a determined, focused, and vigilant effort to see that it does.

CONCLUSION

Trump is no longer in the White House. However, his philosophy about putting every kind of repressive restriction on voting rights to purge millions from the polls is still very much alive and well. No place is it more in play than among the many Trump appointees and GOP-leaning conservative judges on the nation's benches. Judge Lisa Branch, a Trump appointee to the appointee to the 11th Circuit Court demonstrated that in February 2020.

Branch wrote a hard-nosed dissent to a voting rights suit brought by the NAACP against the state of Alabama. She essentially wiped out one of the pillars of the 1965 Voting Rights Act when she ruled individuals can't sue state or local officials who racially discriminate with an election law.

Her dissent flew squarely in the face of the language in

the VRA which permits "an aggrieved person" to bring a voting discrimination suit. It was a dissent, but it was a dissent that Roberts and other conservative SCOTUS jurists almost certainly took keen note of and may lean on when the Act inevitably comes back before the high court.

In truth, Branch's dissent was yet another reflection of one of the GOP's fondest wishes. That is to kill the 1965 Voting Rights Act. Twice it floated several trial balloons in Congress. The first one was in 1981 when the Act came up for renewal. The deal in the initial passage of the Act was that it be renewed every 25 years. The second was in 2006 at the next renewal date. Both Presidents Reagan and Bush ignored congressional conservatives and their administration officials who urged the presidents to refuse to renew or to modify the act.

However, the threats were a forewarning of things to come. In the years since 2006, the drumbeat to do away with the Act and all the protections it afforded has grown to a deafening roar. The GOP uses the same shop-worn arguments that it punishes the South for past voting discrimination sins, it's outmoded and unnecessary and is too intrusive on local election governance.

Meanwhile, the GOP did everything legally possible to erode the Act with the rash of draconian voter restrictive laws that the GOP governors and GOP-controlled state legislatures enacted in recent years. The aim is to discourage and damp down the number of minority and poor voters that overwhelmingly vote Democratic.

Conclusion

It backfired in 2008, 2012, and 2020. Black and Hispanic voters thumbed their noses at the GOP vote suppression ploys and packed the voting booths in mass numbers in those presidential election years. The GOP now faced the looming problem that it could permanently lose its dominant political power and control in the five Deep South states, and other Old Confederacy states.

The GOP's hoped-for ace card to stave that off as long as possible remains the Supreme Court. It upheld the Shelby suit in 2013 which ripped away one of the key enforcement provisions. This gave strong hint that it was just the start of a future dissect of the Voting Rights Act.

Chief Justice Roberts bluntly said that things have changed in the South and that Blacks supposedly vote everywhere in the South without any barriers or prohibitions. Clarence Thomas, to no surprise, went even further and flatly called Section 5 of the Act unconstitutional and left no doubt if, and when, he had the chance, he'd knock the Act out completely.

The repeated claim that the Act is a waste since Blacks and Hispanics vote whenever and wherever they please is nonsense. Even though Black and Hispanic voters did vote in big numbers in the 2012 and the 2020 elections, in many districts they still had to stand in endless lines, have their IDs thoroughly scrutinized, had no bilingual ballots, found voting hours shortened, and had to file legal challenges in state and federal courts to get injunctions to stop the more onerous of the voter suppression laws from being enforced.

This is only part of the story of the roadblocks the GOP almost daily throws up. A study by the Alliance for Justice, a Washington DC-based public interest group documented legions of complaints and challenges filed by the Justice Department and voting rights groups to discriminatory changes that county registrars have made to eliminate or narrow down the number of voters in predominantly minority districts.

With the defeat of Trump and the Democratic control of the House and narrow edge in the Senate, the GOP will beat the voting rights elimination war drums even louder. The old poll tax, literacy tests, and mile length registration forms may be a thing of a bygone shameful racist past. The massive wave of GOP voter suppression laws, rulings, decisions, and maneuvers are very much a part of a very real American presence.

President Biden, Vice President Kamala Harris, and Attorney General Merrick Garland have all made one thing clear. They will fight tooth and nail to beat back the GOP's hit campaign against voting rights. The three have branded the GOP vote suppression campaign, "Jim Crow in the 21st century."

They are right. And the Democrats will need every weapon at their disposal to accomplish that. It will be a hard-fought, vicious, unprecedented knock down drag out prolonged fight—but a fight that must be fought. Nothing less than the democratic right of all citizens to vote is on the line in this monumental fight.

APPENDIX I

KEY PROVISIONS OF THE VOTING RIGHTS ACT OF 1965

The most important permanent provisions of the VRA are Section 2, which bans racial discrimination in voting nationwide, and Sections 4 and 201, which ban literacy tests nationwide.

The most important temporary provisions—provisions that get periodically reauthorized by Congress—are:

- Section 5, which requires certain state and local governments (called "covered jurisdictions") to "preclear" proposed changes in voting or election procedures with either the U.S. Department of Justice or the U.S. District Court for the District of Columbia, and
- Section 203, which requires that certain state and

local jurisdictions provide assistance in languages other than English to voters who are not literate or fluent in English.

- Sections 6-9, which give the U.S. Attorney General the power to send federal examiners and observers to monitor elections.

SECTION 5 OF THE VRA

Preclearance under Section 5 of the Act is defined as those jurisdictions identified under the Act that wanted to change laws and practices affecting voting were required to submit the change along with a letter explaining the change to the Department of Justice.

The jurisdiction must demonstrate that the change does "not have the purpose and will not have the effect of denying or abridging the right to vote on account of race or color

[or membership in a language minority group]." Citizens may submit comments to the Department of Justice on how the proposed change will affect their community. Within 60 days, the department responds either by approving or "preclearing" the change or by objecting to it.

An objection bars the jurisdiction from implementing the proposed change. If an objection is issued and a jurisdiction wishes to appeal, the jurisdiction may seek preclearance through the D.C. District Court. The jurisdiction may alternatively preclear its changes through a lawsuit in the D.C. District Court.

Appendix I

JURISDICTIONS COVERED BY SECTION 5

A formula designed by Congress in Section 4(b) of the VRA applies Section 5 to any state or county where a "test or device" such as a literacy test was used as of November 1, 1964, and where there was a participation rate of under 50 percent by eligible voters in the 1964 presidential election. Later amendments to the Act incorporated participation in the elections of 1968 and 1972 into the coverage formula.

Prior to a 2013 Supreme Court decision, Section 5 affected all or part of 15 states.

- Whole State Covered: Alabama, Alaska, Arizona, Georgia, Louisiana, Mississippi, South Carolina, Texas, and Virginia
- Counties Covered: California (3 counties), Florida (5), New York (3), North Carolina (40) and South Dakota (2)
- Townships Covered: Michigan (2 townships)

SHELBY COUNTY V. HOLDER

The Voting Rights Act has been reauthorized several times by Congress since its initial passage. But on June 25, 2013, the Supreme Court ruled in the case Shelby County v. Holder that the coverage formula in Section 4(b) of the Voting Rights Act, which was used to determine the states and political subdivisions subject to Section 5 preclearance, was unconstitutional.

Thus, while the Court did not invalidate the Section 5 preclearance mechanism in the Voting Rights Act per se, it effectively halted its use by invalidating the formula that determined which jurisdictions were subject to the preclearance obligation, leaving the opportunity for voter suppression tactics to be reintroduced in states that had been previously covered under Section 5 of the VRA.

APPENDIX II

10 KEY PROVISIONS OF HR 1 "FOR THE PEOPLE ACT"

1. Support for D.C. statehood

HR 1 changes a lot of laws, but it also contains nonbinding provisions to express Democrats' support for policies that, for whatever reason, they didn't include in the package. One declares support for D.C. statehood—a matter Congress hasn't voted on since 1993.

"District of Columbia residents deserve full congressional voting rights and self-government, which only statehood can provide," the bill says, adding that "there are no constitutional, historical, financial, or economic reasons why the 700,000 Americans who live in the District of Columbia should not be granted statehood."

2. Presidential transitions and inaugural committees

The overhaul imposes new ethical requirements on presidents and other administration officials, but a lesser-known part of the bill would also establish new rules and prohibitions on their transition teams and inaugural committees.

It would require presidential inaugural committees to disclose expenditures and would put a $50,000-per-person cap on donations to such committees with a requirement for public disclosure within 24 hours of any donations worth $1,000. It would also make it illegal for inaugural committees to solicit, accept or receive donations from "a person that is not an individual," banning corporations and unions from giving to them.

The overhaul would also impose new ethical standards for the presidential transition teams that help the White House and agencies move into power after Election Day. Lobbyists routinely work on these teams, and the bill would prohibit those with "personal financial conflicts of interest" from working on such matters. It also would require each transition team member to sign a "Code of Ethical Conduct."

3. Allowing campaign funds for certain personal expenses

The measure is well-known for its provisions that seek to reduce the role of big-money donors in favor of grassroots contributions, but a less discussed provision would

Appendix II

overhaul the way candidates can use their campaign cash.

Designed to make running for office more accessible to low-income individuals, the provision allows candidates to treat as campaign expenditures personal costs for health insurance, care of their children or other dependents, and any expenses required to maintain a professional license or certification. Spending on those matters would be subject to existing campaign expenditure limits.

4. Registering kids to vote

The bill's requirements that every state offer same-day and automatic voter registration have gotten plenty of attention, but the measure also includes a provision to prepare minors to depart the kids' table for the voting booths. The measure would allow states to start registering minors to vote, as long as they are at least 16 years old.

Republicans have attacked the provision as adding new risks of voting fraud in case the underage crowd tried to vote prematurely. But Democratic supporters argue it's a convenient way to sign up future voters. Meanwhile, the bill would also allow most colleges and universities to become voter registration spots like departments of motor vehicles.

5. Paper ballots

Though the measure puts new regulations on online advertisements and new requirements for election cybersecurity, it has something for those who might feel nostalgic for the old days of paper ballots.

That's right, the overhaul requires the use of "durable, voter-verified" paper ballots in federal elections, according to legislative text.

6. Prepaid postage for absentee ballots

Voting absentee is probably less of a hassle for most people than going to the polls, but the legislation seeks to make that process easier by providing prepaid postage for absentee ballots in federal elections.

Practically speaking, that means voters would not need to find a stamp to mail in their absentee ballot for presidential or midterm elections, as the state or local government that administers the ballot will be on the hook for the postage.

7. Crime to mislead voters

While well known for provisions to make voting access easier, the bill also makes it a crime for people who, within 60 days of an election, provide false information to voters with the intention of misleading them or preventing them from voting.

For example, the provision would make it illegal to intentionally lie to people about the time and place a polling location is open or about their eligibility to vote. The crime should carry a penalty of up to five years in prison, a maximum fine of $100,000, or both, the bill says.

8. Clamping down on foreign influence

Appendix II

After the 2016 elections brought intense focus on possible foreign interference, it's no surprise House Democrats included provisions to overhaul the Foreign Agents Registration Act. They'll also vote on whether to impose new limits on the political spending of companies with at least a 5 percent foreign government owner or companies with at least a 20 percent foreign national owner.

Representatives for corporations say they are concerned about foreign-national provisions potentially hitting even the political action committees of businesses with just one foreign national shareholder. Supporters of the bill say those fears are unfounded.

9. Large websites to record political advertisers

The measure is full of transparency provisions, mostly to force the government to bring more of its operations into the sunshine. But one provision seeks to make online platforms that accept political ads to be more transparent by requiring public-facing websites with 50 million or more unique visitors a month to maintain a record of advertisers whose aggregate purchase requests exceed $500 per year.

This provision, which would affect social media companies such as Facebook that accept political advertisements, is designed to let the public know who is trying to influence elections.

10. Posting congressional reports online

Another overlooked but significant transparency

provision would require online public disclosure of congressionally mandated reports, such as those from federal agencies or the Congressional Research Service, dubbed the think tank for lawmakers.

* * * * *

Most CRS reports have already been made available online, as required by a provision in the fiscal 2018 omnibus bill. But agency reports to Congress are not often made public, unless the agency or the lawmaker or committee who requested the report chooses to release it.

NOTES

Chris Hymes, "Attorney general announces actions to protect voting rights" www.msn.com/en-us/news/politics/attorney-general-announces-actions-to-protect-voting-rights/ar-AAKXlEj, CBS News, June 9, 2021

Reality Check Team, "US election 2020: Fact-checking Trump team's main fraud claims," BBC, November 23, 2020 www.bbc.com/news/election-us-2020-55016029

Alex Woodward, "What is HR1 and what would the bill mean for voting rights?" Independent, May 11, 2020 www.news.yahoo.com/hr1-bill-mean-voting-rights-171440929.html
www.independent.co.uk/news/world/americas/us-politics/for-the-people-act-democrats-b1812180.html

Reagan McCarthy, "McConnell Slams HR 1's 'Federal Takeover of Elections," Townhall, March 3, 2021 www.townhall.com/tipsheet/reaganmccarthy/2021/03/24/mcconnell-on-hr1-n2586757

Brennan Center, "Debunking the Voter Fraud Myth, " www.brennancenter.org/sites/default/files/analysis/Briefing_Memo_Debunking_Voter_Fraud_Myth.pdf
www.brennancenter.org/analysis/analysis-noncitizen-voting-vanishingly-rare.

Additional resources can be found here:
www.brennancenter.org/analysis/analysis-andreports
www.news.yahoo.com/gop-lawmakers-push-voting-law-122849876.html

John Celock, "Kris Kobach, Kansas Secretary Of State, Seeks Power To Prosecute Voter Fraud," Huff Post, 11/30/2012 www.huffpost.com/entry/kris-kobach-voter-fraud_n_2219492

Brayan Lowry and Hunter Woodall, "Trump disbands Kobach-led voter fraud commission after resistance from states," Kansas City Star, January 3, 2018
www.kansascity.com/news/politics-government/article192854444.html
"U.S. Associate Attorney General Vanita Gupta on the right to protect voting rights," Yahoo News, June 13, 2021

www.news.yahoo.com/u-associate-attorney-general-vanita-171335077.html

Axios, "Attorney General Garland to promise voting-rights fight in major policy speech," Yahoo News, June 11, 2021 www.news.yahoo.com/attorney-general-garland-promise-voting-114153844.html

Ronald Brownstein, "The 'urban myth' behind the GOP claims of voter fraud," CNN, December 15, 2020 www.cnn.com/2020/12/15/politics/voter-fraud-urban-myth/index.html

Earl Ofari Hutchinson, "GOP Steps Up Bogus War on Voter Fraud," Huff Post, June 4, 2012 www.huffpost.com/entry/gop-steps-up-bogus-war-on_b_1566881

Nicole Carroll, "Backstory: We investigated claims of voter fraud in the election. Here's what we found," USA Today, November 13, 2020
www.usatoday.com/story/opinion/2020/11/13/trump-voter-fraud-claims-investigated-2020-election/6259980002/
upreme Court upholds voter ID law

AP, "Supreme Court Upholds Voter ID Law, ", NBC News, April 28, 2008
www.nbcnews.com/id/wbna24351798

Mississippi Voter Application and Literacy Test ~ 1950s
www.crmvet.org/info/ms-littest55.pdf

National Archives, "Voting Rights in the Early 1960s: "Registering Who They Wanted To"
http://rediscovering-black-history.blogs.archives.gov/2016/10/25/voting-rights-in-the-early-1960s-registering-who-they-wanted-to/

Alan Greenblatt, "The Racial History Of The 'Grandfather Clause, " NPR, October 21, 2013
www.npr.org/sections/codeswitch/2013/10/21/239081586/the-racial-history-of-the-grandfather-clause

"Disfranchisement after the Reconstruction era," Wikipedia, nd https://en.wikipedia.org/wiki/Disfranchisement_after_the_Reconstruction_era
www.abcnews.go.com/Politics/timeline-voter-suppression-us-civil-war-today/story?id=72248473

Jessica Bursztynsky, "Major U.S. companies take aim at Georgia's new voting restrictions," CNBC, March 3, 2021
www.cnbc.com/2021/03/31/major-us-companies-take-aim-at-georgias-new-voting-restrictions.html

Travis Waldron, "Republican State Legislatures Are Winning Their War On American Democracy," Huff Post, June 6, 2021 www.huffpost.com/entry/republican-voting-rights-democracy_n_60ba544ee4b04b216be68ce6

V R. Newkirk III, "Voter Suppression Is Warping Democracy," The Atlantic, July 17, 2018 www.theatlantic.com/politics/archive/2018/07/poll-prri-voter-suppression/565355/

Walker Bragman, "Corporations Are Still Funding the GOP Campaign to Roll Back Voting Rights," Jacobin, May 27, 2021 www.jacobinmag.com/2021/05/voter-suppression-capitol-riot-chamber-commerce

Ken Tenbarge, "In leaked audio, a top Trump adviser said the Republican party has 'traditionally' relied on voter suppression," Business Insider, December 21, 2019 www.businessinsider.com/leaked-audio-trump-adviser-republicans-rely-voter-suppression-justin-clark-2019-12

Alex Henderson, "Republican AG admits voter suppression helped Trump win Texas in 2020, Alternet, June 8, 2021 www.alternet.org/2021/06/ken-paxton/

Herb Denton, "Reagan signs Voter Rights extension, " Washington Post , June 30, 1982 www.washingtonpost.com/archive/politics/1982/06/30/reagan-signs-voting-rights-act-extension/b59370f1-fc93-4e2f-b417-2b614ea55910/

Ian Millhiser, "Chief Justice Roberts's lifelong crusade against voting rights, explained," Vox, September 18, 2020 www.msn.com/en-us/news/politics/chief-justice-roberts-s-lifelong-crusade-against-voting-rights-explained/ar-BB19aW31

The Heritage Foundation, "The Facts About H.R. 1: The "For the People Act of 2021" www.heritage.org/election-integrity/report/the-facts-about-hr-1-the-the-people-act-2021

Congresss.gov, "H.R.1 - For the People Act of 2019," www.congress.gov/bill/116th-congress/house-bill/1/text#toc-H67D4FBDA0E0747BE8E6548AA184D330F

P.R. Lockhart, "Florida Legislature approves bill requiring former felons to pay fines and fees before voting," Vox, May 3, 2019
www.vox.com/policy-and-politics/2019/5/3/18528564/amendment-4-florida-felon-voting-rights-fees

Matt Apuzzo, "Holder Urges States to Lift Bans on Felons," NY Times, February 12, 2014
www.nytimes.com/2014/02/12/us/politics/holder-urges-states-to-repeal-bans-on-voting-by-felons.html

Tom Liddy, "Donald Trump Says Electoral College 'Genius' After Calling It 'Disaster." ABC News, November 15, 2016 www.abcnews.go.com/US/donald-trump-electoral-college-genius-calling-disaster/story?id=43564890

Earl Ofari Hutchinson," Why Should Trump Disavow Racists, If the GOP Cannot?," The Immigrant Magazine, March 6, 2016
www.immigrantmagazine.com/why-should-trump-disavow-racists-if-the-gop-cannot/

Shusshana Walshe, "RNC Completes 'Autopsy' on 2012 Loss, Calls for Inclusion Not Policy Change, ABC News, March 18, 2013
www.abcnews.go.com/Politics/OTUS/rnc-completes-autopsy-2012-loss-calls-inclusion-policy/story?id=18755809

Rebecca Sinderbrand, "Analysis: Obama won with a better ground game," CNN, November 7, 2012
www.cnn.com/2012/11/07/politics/analysis-why-obama-won/index.html

Natalie Brown, "How Stacey Abrams Helped Joe Biden win Georgia, news.com. November 6, 2020,
www.news.com.au/world/north-america/us-politics/us-election-2020-how-stacey-abrams-helped-joe-biden-win-georgia/news-story/a283ccb87ef520de3eeef2b12bf65b05

Mark Joseph Stern, "Trump Judge Argues Voters Can't Sue States Over Voting Rights," Slate, February 4, 2020 www.slate.com/news-and-politics/2020/02/trump-judge-voters-sue-voting-rights-act.html

Axios, "Attorney General Garland to promise voting-rights fight in major policy speech," Yahoo News, June 11, 2021 www.news.yahoo.com/attorney-general-garland-promise-voting-114153844.html

APPENDIX I
www.yourvoteyourvoicemn.org/key-provisions-voting-rights-act-1965

APPENDIX II
HR 1 Appendix 2
www.rollcall.com/2019/03/06/10-things-you-might-not-know-about-hr-1/

BIBLIOGRAPHY

Alexander, Michelle, *The New Jim Crow* (The New Press, 2012)

Bell C., Richard, *Voting: The Ultimate Act of Resistance: The Real Truth from the Voting Rights Battlefields*, (Word Association Publishers, 2020

Branch, Taylor, *Pillar of Fire; America in the King Years 1963-1965* (Simon & Schuster, 1998)

Burgan, Michael, *The Voting Rights Act of 1965: An Interactive History Adventure* (You Choose: History) (Capstone Press, 2015)

Hasen, Richard L., *The Voting Wars: From Florida 2000 to the Next Election Meltdown* (Yale Univ. Press, 2012)

Hutchinson, Earl Ofari, *Betrayed; a History of the Presidential Failure to Protect Black Lives* (Westview Press, 1996)

Keyssar, Alexander, T*he Right To Vote: The Contested History of Democracy in the United States* (Basic Books, 2000)

Klarman, Michael J., *From Jim Crow to Civil Rights: The Supreme Court and the Struggle for Racial Equality* (Oxford University Press, 2006)

Lansford, Tom (ed.), *Voting Rights (Opposing Viewpoints)* (Greenhaven, 2008)

Lawson, Stephen F., *Black Ballots: Voting Rights in the South, 1944-1969* (Lexington Books, 1999)

Mann, Robert, *The Walls of Jericho, Lyndon Johnson, Hubert Humphrey, Richard Russell and the struggle for civil rights* (Harcourt Brace, 1996)

Ogletree. Jr., Charles J., *All Deliberate Speed: Reflections on the First Half Century of Brown v. Board of Education* (W.W. Norton, 2004)

Riser Volney, R. *Defying Disfranchisement: Black Voting Rights Activism in the Jim Crow South, 1890-1908* (LSU Press, 2010)

Roth, Zachary, *The Great Suppression: Voting Rights, Corporate Cash, and the Conservative Assault on Democracy* (Crown, 2016)

Zelden, Charles L., *Voting Rights on Trial* (Hackett, 2004)

Zelden, Charles L., *Bush v. Gore: Exposing the Hidden Crisis in American Democracy* (U. Press of Kansas, 2008

Zelden, Charles L., T*he Battle for the Black Ballot: Smith v. Allwright and the Defeat of the Texas All-White Primary* (U. Press of Kansas, 2005)

INDEX

Abrams, Stacey, 82
African American voters, 111-12, 43,50, 55, 58-59, 85, 96-87, 102
    Jim Crow disfranchisement, 25-26
African American elected officials ,52
Asian Voters, 85
Biden, Joe, 1, 8, 43, 56, 81, 104
    Legislative initiatives, 3
Booker, Cory, 79
Brennan Center, 8-9, 29, 40, 67
    Voting fraud debunked, 8-9
Bush Jr., George, 57, 58
Bush-Gore 2000 Presidential Election, 3, 19, 69
Capitol riot (January 6), 2, 13, 34, 90
Carlson, Tucker, 7-8
Clinton, Hillary, 83, 85
Congress, 51, 103, 77, 104

Conyers, John, 77
Conservative media, 15
Democrats, 3, 15 ,19 ,21, 50, 62, 66, 81-82, 103
Department of Justice, 10, 18, 48, 49, 104
Electoral College, 83-88
Felon voting ban, 71-78
    Florida vote ban initiative, 71
Fox News, 4
Garland, Merrick, 5, 104
GOP, 1, 2-3, 14, 15, 35, 40, 56-57
    Political action groups, 2
Political dominance, 2, 13, 29, 58
    SCOTUS ruling, 56-57
    Felon voting ban, 73
    Racism, 91
White voters, 91
    Vote suppression tactics 4-5, 8, 9, 13, 19, 29, 58, 68-69, 87-88, 101-104
Gerrymandering, 28-29
Grandfather clause, 26
Harris, Kamala, 104
Harris County Mail in Ballot, 43-44
Hispanic voters, 18, 43, 58-59, 103, 104, 105
Holder, Eric, 57, 68,70,71,74,77
HR 1 For the People Act, 3, 4, 21, 59, 62, 98-99
Johnson, Lyndon B., 64, 65
Kemp, Brian, 33, 34, 56, 80
Kosbach, Kris, 10
    Georgia voter suppression law, 34-35
Lewis, John, 61-62
Literacy Tests, 24-25, 40
    Mississippi literarcy test, 24
Major corporations, vote suppression, 33-38
McConnell, Mitch, 2, 3, 4, 62, 90

Index

Nixon, Richard, 50
North Carolina same day voting elimination, 41, 52
Nineteenth Amendment, 26
Obama, Barack, 3, 30, 57, 63, 68, 69, 91
Poll Tax, 23-24
Priebus, Reince, 89, 90
Republican National Lawyers Assn., 70
Republican Attorneys General Assn., 35
Roberts, John, 40, 49, 54, 61, 99, 102, 103
    Memo opposing VRA, 49
Scalia, Antonin, 52
SCOTUS, 26, 37, 39, 41, 55, 81
Scott, Rick, 18
    Florida voter purge, 18
Selma Edmund Pettus Bridge, 68
Shelby v. Holder, 39, 41, 49-50, 60, 102
Student voter ID law, 20
Texas AG, Ken Paxton, 43
Texas voter ID law, 31, 30, 61, 70
Trump, Donald, 1, 2, 3, 12, 13, 14, 30, 63, 83, 85, 87
    Birther attack Obama, 14
    Presidential Advisory Committee on Election Integrity, 10
    Vote fraud claim (tweet), 1
    Racism, 13
USA Today vote fraud fact check, 16-17, 18
Voting Rights Act, 5, 21, 22, 26, 39, 45, 59, 61, 64-66, 68, 102
    VRA extension, 48

ABOUT EARL OFARI HUTCHINSON

Earl Ofari Hutchinson is the author of multiple books on race and politics in America. He is a political analyst. He has appeared on MSNBC and on CNN. His books include the trilogy on the Obama Years: The Obama Legacy, How Obama Governed; The Year of Crisis and Challenge, and How Obama Won. His most recent books are the Trump Challenge to Black America, From King to Obama: Witness to a Turbulent History. He is the publisher of thehutchinsonreport.net, a political issues web blog.

www.ingramcontent.com/pod-product-compliance
Lightning Source LLC
Chambersburg PA
CBHW030442010526
44118CB00011B/754